BROTHER JOHN

LOVESICK

PUBLISHED by PARABLE
Earthly Stories with a Heavenly Meaning

Pathways To The Past

Each volume stands alone as an Individual Book
Each volume stands together with others
to enhance the value of your collection

Build your Personal, Pastoral or Church Library
Pathways To The Past contains an ever-expanding list of
Christendom's most influencial authors

Augustine of Hippo
Athanasius
E. M. Bounds
John Bunyan
Brother Lawrence
Jessie Penn-Lewis
Bernard of Clairvaux
Andrew Murray
Watchman Nee
Arthur W. Pink
Hannah Whitall Smith
R. A. Torrey
A. W. Tozer
Jean-Pierre de Caussade
Thomas Watson
And many, many more.

Tiitle: Lovesick
Brother John Foy
Rights: All Rights Reserved
ISBN 978-1-945698-06-4
Doctrinal theology, Inspiration
Salvation, Dicipleship, Spiritual Warfare
Other books by this author include: Why Are The Fishermen Eating The Bait?

Brother John

LOVESICK

PUBLISHED by PARABLE
Earthly Stories with a Heavenly Meaning

Author's Preface

This book is intended to help any and all who read it to be able to follow it and become all they can be to become mature sons and daughters of God. Having been involved in evangelism, discipleship and Bible schools, it is my heart that those being mentored become like Elisha and do more, go further and experience more of God than I could ever have imagined. This book is a response to that question I had as a young believer, "How do I get there?" That question may have been defined differently for different sects of Christianity but for many there seems to be a sense that there was more and that the Bible contained the answer. How to do what needs to be done and knowing wha needs to be done – that was my dilemma. I believe that the Bible tells us the end goal for each individual believer and for the Church as a whole. Jesus is the bride groom and He is returning for a pure, sanctified and consecrated bride, not a dirty, beat up, idol worshiping bride.

    I found in my Christian walk that there were many books that taught subjects about God but after reading these book I would often leave with a feeling that something was missing – there seemed to be a missing part. I found myself filled with a desire to find this missing part and to know why and how to deepen my relationship with Christ. Books are great and helpful. They can teach you someone's lifelong lessons in a matter of minutes and after a short time you can begin to experience change. But without the correct foundation you will not be a stable and strong temple. Often I would hear preachers speak about something and see many people jump right into the Christian lifestyle and they did not have the foundation. Many did not last, or if they did, they are caught up in the business of church and powerless lifestyle. They bring with them the standards of the World and how the world does it. They are missing the manifest power of Christianity and the true nature of being a Christian.

It is easy for someone to get saved and begin to walk in niceness, kindness and politeness, which is often viewed as successful Christian living. Those who embrace that brand of Christianity will not survive the battles of life. They will find themselves outside the door when the Groom comes. They lack the marks of the Christian death, the success of Christian character, the presence of God, and more. We need to disciple to convert not convert to disciple. (When and where the Gospel has been preached already) There is a difference and a need for what I am writing about in this book. We must re-lay the foundation that was once lain and then build on it. Being a Christian is not about getting to go to heaven or escaping hell. It is about becoming Christ-like. We're not talking about being a Christian as modern Christianity, or the media, or the world has defined it.

How can you go from being a new Christian, a baby, to becoming a mature son and daughter? How can you become what you hear rumors and stories about? What is that type of person supposed to be doing in the last days? Not running from someone (antichrist) that is for sure. How can you be a partaker of the blessing of God the right way? To seek the blessing of God without the right relationship is treating God like a prostitute. Some seek the highest form of God's blessing without the highest relationship with God. I prefer the latter, and if the former comes, great, but I prefer the God of the blessing.

I do not suppose to know it all, I am far from where I have pointed my life and am heading. Even as I finish these chapters I find myself going deeper and finding more than I could have imagined. I have provided a lot of scripture here for your reference but have not provided all. Please, as you read this, dig in, figure it out for yourself. My revelation and teaching does you no good if you do not know Him personally, nor if you do not make it your own in prayer and study. Please enjoy and please fulfill your destiny!

The Mystery Of God

Job 11:7
"Can you discover the depths of God?

There is a depth of intimacy that is possible with God. It is a depth that has not been explored by many. It is easy to see in scripture that some have met with God. Often it is stated "they walked with God." For years I wondered how this could be possible. Is it possible? Why do the words of Jesus seem so real to me but when I lift up my eyes I see something different? Is it possible to walk with God? Is it possible to fellowship with God like the men of old? Is it still possible to be a mighty man of valor? How can we do it? Is intimacy with God really possible? How do you describe something that is so personal and intimate to you that others would want to be a part of it? Then again why would we want people to be in our intimate affairs? Paul used the example of marriage between a man and a woman to describe how our relationship with Christ should be.

Ephesians 5
31 For this cause shall a man leave his father and mother, and shall be joined unto his wife, and they two shall be one flesh. 32 This is a great mystery: but I speak concerning Christ and the church. 33 Nevertheless let every one of you in particular so love his wife even as himself; and the wife see that she reverence her husband.

He called it a great mystery. Can we understand or figure out what the mystery of Christ is? Can we understand the meaning of "Christ and the Church"? Paul did not go into detail about what a husband and wife experience but he gave us the clue.

How else can you relate something so intimate to others when there are so few examples in human existence to explain it? The closest Paul came to it was a marriage. The intimacy and relationship that a man and woman have is similar to the relationship between you and God. God tells us that we become one with a man or woman when we lay with them. Hopefully that behind doors relationship is based on a love relationship and not just a fling. Do we as a church entertain God as a fling? You see you cannot communicate with someone you do not trust, nor can you have faith in someone you do not personally know. Our relationship with the creator of the universe is not about a letter of the law or a contract like a marriage contract, but rather it is comparable to the intimate moments of marriage between a man and a woman behind closed doors. It is holy, sacred and indescribable. Often you cannot find the words to tell others why you love someone, you just do. They have touched you in that manner that only you and they can explain. As a man I have heard many men talk about how they met their wives, how they proposed and what the wedding was like. Women will go into great detail about every event leading up to and after the wedding. We invite witnesses to be a part of the ceremony, but not what happens behind closed doors. I have never heard another person talk about what happens after the door closed. It is no one else's business. Our relationship with God is the same way. We may fumble, laugh, cry, whisper, shout, etc... Whatever our reaction and experience it is very personal. It is unique and so personal we do not share it. When we come out of the room we are different and sooner or later we produce fruit, offspring. The husband and wife begin to build a life together. God wants that kind of relationship with you. It is a holy sacred moment between two individuals. God wants to know you and be one with you. It is a holy and sacred event.

We all have personalities that are different and we will all relate to God in individual ways, most ways are the same through prayer, praise and worship, and study of the Word, but beyond those you get intimate with Him. Being alone with Him reveals things no one else ever knew about you. This is the type of knowing that Jesus referred to when he stated in

Matthew 7

21 Not everyone that saith unto me, Lord, Lord, shall enter into the kingdom of heaven; but he that doeth the will of my Father which is in heaven. 22 Many will say to me in that day, Lord, Lord, have we not prophesied in thy name? and in thy name have cast out devils? and in thy name done many wonderful works? 23 And then will I profess unto them, I never knew you: depart from me, ye that work iniquity.

That knowing is an intimate relational knowing. You cannot just read His love letter and think you have it all figured out. Your relationship would be missing something. You need to have a personal encounter with God every day if possible. You cannot just read love letters, lovers have to get intimate and personal at some point. Otherwise it is just knowledge, no knowing. He created us for fellowship and Love, He is love, and He gave you a portion of that love when you were born again and He wants to water it and feed it. You submit to the process and He will make it grow. As Jesus said, even if it is as small as a mustard seed it can grow to be among the biggest of trees. That growth does not happen on its own but as we submit to His ways and delve into and deepen our relationship with Him. That love that was shed abroad in your heart is waiting there like a dormant seed in need of water, food and love to make it grow. Funny thing is that we can only submit ourselves to His way of doing things and He makes that seed grow. It seems as if the closer we allow Him to get the more that seed responds within us to become more like Him. I once heard a phrase, "Gods looking for God in you!" He created us, saved us, planted a seed in us, and only he can make it grow. We turn ourselves over to Him and He makes it grow.

This personal relationship is required to make the seed grow, mature and produce fruit. Have you ever noticed that the older a couple gets and the longer they have been married, they sound alike, act alike and sometimes ever look alike. They eat together, sleep, travel, hang out, talk and do so much together they act like each other. They have become the same in a way. They have built a life together and they have become one.

This book is a study to a degree of that personal relationship and maybe you could say an introduction into why it works the way it does. It is not mean to be a formula. There is not formula to a personal relationship with God or anyone else for that matter. Yes men are built to desire respect and women are built to desire love. These are basic human needs. How each obtains the meeting of these needs and to what level is different for each person. Things my wife and I do for fun and enjoyment as a couple are not going to be the same for another couple. My relationship with God is individually different than my wife's relationship with God. It will be the same for you. The issue is the relationship.

Giving a Foothold and Becoming a Habitation

There are a number of words in the original languages of the Word that are used only in the English as Love (or expression of love). If you study this out in the Aramaic, Hebrew and the Greek, you will find that there are at least 30 different original words used as Love in the English.

Some have good meanings and some like agabah are not so good. Agabah means inordinate affection. Used in Ezekiel 33
\

Ezekiel 33

30 Also, thou son of man, the children of thy people still are talking against thee by the walls and in the doors of the houses, and speak one to another, everyone to his brother, saying, Come, I pray you, and hear what is the word that cometh forth from the Lord. 31 And they come unto thee as the people cometh, and they sit before thee as my people, and they hear thy words, but they will not do them: for with their mouth they shew much love, but their heart goeth after their covetousness. 32 And, lo, thou art unto them as a very lovely song of one that hath a pleasant voice, and can play well on an instrument: for they hear thy words, but they do them not. 33 And when this cometh to pass, (lo, it will come,) then shall they know that a prophet hath been among them.

Here is a list of some of those words that translate into one or two

English words and variation of the word Love. Examples would be love, lover, to love, be love, brotherly love, love of a wife, etc...

Ahabah, ahabim, dod, rayah, agape, aheb, chabah, racham, agapao, thelo, phileo, aheb, chashaq, agabah, agabim, philoproteuo, rachamim, philadelphia, philadelphos, philarguria, philotjnos, philandros, philantroapia, machmad, prosphiles, agabim, agab, agah, rea, philotheos, philagathos, philautos, philedonos, yadid, ahabim, tob, chesed.

Some of those words are only used once in the original texts, some used a number of times. We are going to focus for the most part in this study on two words. Agape and Agapao

Most teachers and preachers, teach two types. Using John 21 and the story about the restoration of Peter, they teach that there are two types of love, Phileo and Agape.

John 21:15

15 So when they had dined, Jesus saith to Simon Peter, Simon, son of Jonas, lovest thou me more than these? He saith unto him, Yea, Lord; thou knowest that I love thee. He saith unto him, Feed my lambs. 16 He saith to him again the second time, Simon, son of Jonas, lovest thou me? He saith unto him, Yea, Lord; thou knowest that I love thee. He saith unto him, Feed my sheep. 17 He saith unto him the third time, Simon, son of Jonas, lovest thou me? Peter was grieved because he said unto him the third time, Lovest thou me? And he said unto him, Lord, thou knowest all things; thou knowest that I love thee. Jesus saith unto him, Feed my sheep.

Peter used the word Phileo, Jesus used the word Agape, twice and then dropped down to the word Phileo the third time and then Peter realized what Jesus was saying. Jesus was saying, "Do you love me as God loves you?" Peter kept saying, "I love you like a friend or a brother". When we get to the end of this exchange we find that Peter finally comes to realize that Jesus is referring to something greater than brotherly love. Peter was shamed but he got the point. Jesus was even referring to something greater than just walking in love. He was trying to get Peter to realize that Peter had to become love.

Most will say that the word Phileo refers to the man kind of love, and Agape refers to the God kind of love. While this is basically correct, the rabbit hole can and does go further. One will produce man's results and the other will produce God's kind of results. One produces the fruits of the flesh as listed in Galatians 5:19-20 while the other produces the fruit of Galatians 5:22.

But there is another Greek word that is used throughout the New Testament that is very similar to the Agape kind of love. It is the action of love. It is the verb of love. It is Agapao

Agapao is use throughout the Word of God (New Testament), it is translated as love or to love. If you do not study the two words Agape and Agapao (as well as the others) you will go around thinking that the meaning of love is all the same. But these two very popularly used words in the Greek New Testament are not the same. They both relate to the God kind of love but they are very different.

Romans 13:8-9

8 Owe no man anything, but to love one another: for he that loveth another hath fulfilled the law. 9 For this, Thou shalt not commit adultery, Thou shalt not kill, Thou shalt not steal, Thou shalt not bear false witness, Thou shalt not covet; and if there be any other commandment, it is briefly comprehended in this saying, namely, Thou shalt love thy neighbour as thyself. 10 Love worketh no ill to his neighbour: therefore love is the fulfilling of the law.

In verse 8 we see the word love and then again in verse 10. But they are not the same.

In verse 8 the word is Agapeo, the action, the practice, the conduct of love. We could say that this is the verb of love. We would use this word to describe the way love acts. I call it the practicing or the demonstration of God's love.

If you were to begin in life as a young man or women and decide, "Hey I want to be a carpenter". You would go get a job and begin learning the trade. You do not know everything from day one, and you may even be a quick learner. Most who want to be a carpenter, (or any trade, profession) would spend years learning the trade. Learning the fundamentals of carpentry, learning the carpenter's way of doing -- this is essential. Most likely you would get a job working for a carpenter. Learning all you can from them and developing your trade. You make mistakes; you get stretched and pulled as you learn. You are in a sense on a journey. One who is learning a trade, but not yet ready to be out on your own. But as the years go by and as you develop as tradesmen, you become a carpenter. One day you are ready to step out on your own and now people even refer to you as a carpenter. You no longer work for or as a carpenter, but you have become a carpenter.

This word used here in Romans 8, has that kind of meaning with it. Agapao is the action, the trade of Love. It is the business of love, it is the word that describes the way love works and develops. It describes the actions we associate with the trade of Love. It is the practice and demonstration of Love. It is a verb that describes the act or practice of loving others.

If you want to be an athlete you do not show up and win races from day one. Probably most "wanna be" athletes have to begin as the least of the team. They have to prove themselves and slowly as they grow and train they begin to compete, then they begin to win, then one day they are no longer wanting to be an athlete but they are one. People would introduce you to others as an athlete. You are no longer just practicing but being. You went from wanting and acting like it and learning the skills and aspects of something but now you are that which you desired to be. You became what you followed after and desired.

In Verse 10, we see the word love, but it is not the same as verse 8. This word in the Greek is AGAPE. The noun, the person, the substance of Love. It is the person, the nature of Love. Here we see our carpenter went from learning, acting and training in love, but now has reached the position, the being of love. This is the love that has become what they trained for. You are no longer a lover in training, but you have become Love. You went from being a verb to becoming a noun. You became that which you pursued. You went from being Agapao to Agape. You have gone from practicing to becoming the nature of Love. This is why we walk in love -- to become love. As you walk in it daily, practicing and demonstrating God's Love to the rest of the world in how we treat others, you end up becoming what you imitated!

Notice in verse 10, he uses the words, His Neighbor. Why would he refer to HIS? Who is that word referring to? LOVE. Agape. A pronoun. You see you start out walking in the precepts, the action and the rules of Agapao love only to end up becoming Agape love. You become that which you have practiced!

Think about it like this. Ephesians 4:7 says, do not give the devil a foot hold. If you do it has the potential to ruin you. Also 2 Timothy 2:26, he refers to the snare of the devil. If we give the devil a place he will use it to attempt to ruin us. He only comes to kill, steal, and destroy. If you give him a foothold and he will drag you down to the end of his game, the end of sin, which is death.

God is not that way. If you give God a foot hold, He will develop you into an image of Him and His love. He will produce in you His desire. You being to walk in the light you have and as you allow it and pursue it, you become it. If you will allow Him to, He will deposit that nature, that blueprint in you and then if you submit to His way He will transform you into the image of Himself in this earth. You go from being a Christian to becoming lie Christ.

It works in the natural world as well as the spiritual realm, positively and negatively...

I know for myself, I was introduced to alcohol this way. I went to a party with a bunch of classmates. I was not one of them, but as I sat there that night and I so badly wanted to be accepted and loved, they acted as if they wanted me around. Then the next week I did it again. Then more and more and after going into the military it developed into a way of life for me to spend Friday and Saturday night out at the bars. Finally is got to the point that I was out 5 nights a week, drinking and acting a fool. Then one day I heard someone say, "Are you an alcoholic?" You see I had given the devil foot hood and it did its job, and while I started out just acting like others and learning from them, it got me. I went from a foothold, to a way of life, a habit and then finally a habitation. I had become what I had practiced for years and it had a hold of me.

It is the same way with any smoker, drug user, etc. The foothold that you allow, for whatever reason or for whatever need you are trying to fill, that foothold will become a way of life, then a habit and sooner or later if something does not deliver you, it becomes a habitation. You are an addict as we say.

God deals with us in a similar way. People who just hang around the edges of the church never really get into it. They stay that way. Socialites, but you find someone who decided to begin studying the Word and pursuing God they become something else. They give God a foot hold, which becomes more as they study and develop in Him. It becomes a way of life, a habit. But God wants to become a habitation in you. He wants to take up residency in you. He wants to possess you in and out. This is not just practicing the God kind of love, but you become Love. This is what verse 10 refers too.

Read it with those words exchanged for the Greek meaning

8 Owe no man anything, but to walk in love and practice love for one another: for he that acts and demonstrates love for another hath fulfilled the law. 9 For this, Thou shalt not commit adultery, Thou shalt not kill, Thou shalt not steal, Thou shalt not bear false witness, Thou shalt not covet; and if there be any other commandment, it is briefly comprehended in this saying, namely, Thou shalt demonstrate and practice love thy neighbor as thyself. 10 THE PERSON OF LOVE worketh no ill to his neighbor: therefore YOU THE BEING OF LOVE, THE MANIFEST PRESENCE OF LOVE is the fulfilling of the law.

We can argue the finer point all night, but the thing is this, God is Love and God is a Spirit, therefore we are not taking a large leap to say the Spirit is Love. It the Spirit of Love dwells in you, should you not reflect Love? Not just things of the Spirit, the gifts of the Spirit, but the manifest presence of the Spirit of God is and it should be Love. That is why Paul said, "Let me show you the more excellent way". Love. All else can fail but Love cannot. In searching the scriptures, I have found 4 things that cannot fail. God, His mercy, His Word and Love. You cannot change any of those but you can practice Mercy and Love. You can follow after Love and stay in Love, You can have mercy on others and not shut up the bowels of Mercy within you. You can love with no strings attached and become that which you practice. I believe Paul found the real secret when He said, "follow after love"! Or in Galatians, "the only thing that matters is faith expressing itself in Love"!

Love is not to me a topic that should be preached once in a while as it is just a minor topic, but I see everything in the scriptures in light of the Love of God. I want every sermon to include, the love of God and Jesus. Name me a topic and I will bring it back to love. Love is the key to all that we do, without it we are still lost. It is the thing that makes Christianity more than a religion but a relationship. God so loved that He gave us His Son and His Spirit, if we chose to accept them. Forgiveness and giving are two key character traits of Agape and Agapao, as well as holiness and truthfulness. To say you are walking in love and yet do things the Holy Spirit would not be a part of is to be deceived.

You see the Holy Spirit is not some Casper type of ghost that floats around looking for someone to join up with. He is the Spirit of God, the part of God's being that is at work in the World today, but He is also the Spirit of Love. You will never hear the Spirit of God say something apart from Love. The Voice of the Spirit is the voice of Love. It may bring correction, it may bring discipline, but it is always Love.

I have met so many former preachers. As I talk with them I find that they got disgruntled, disillusioned and unsatisfied with Christianity. When we get to the heart of the matter, there was never a foundation of love or relationship to propel them. It was a job, it was a career, it was powerless, impersonal and lonely. They entered into ministry and never had the personal intimate relationship with God to keep them there. They had no foundation in knowing God, the God of Love. They never knew God as the person of the Holy Spirit. You cannot endure the trials and tribulations of this world without the Comforter. He is our Coach, our Guide and the One who we can depend on. Without a relationship with Him, life is not worth living. The Holy Spirit is the one who brings the Word to life in our hearts, who reveals wisdom to us as He is the Spirit of Wisdom. He operates through us and with us to accomplish what He asks us to do.

He is the Spirit of Love and as John the Baptist stated, He must increase and I must decrease, the Holy Spirit of Love must increase and the flesh and carnal man we are must decrease. Let Him come in, let Him take over and let Him make you into what your heart desires but your brain is ignorant to. Love cannot fail, The Spirit of Love cannot fail. If He resides in you and you give Him the chance, you will not fail!

The Spirit of Love the Holy Spirit will lead you into the God kind of life. He will lead you into holiness, love and the gifts of the Spirit. We must develop the relationship with the Spirit of God to become like Him. It will lead you into all things, He will teach you all things. To walk in love is to be separate and consecrated to God. You cannot keep testing the waters to determine if you want go back in. Come out from the world and do not look back. I struggled with this for some time as a younger man. I did not understand the need for separation and holiness. I did not understand the purity of the Love of God. God will not allow sin in His presence and the Holy Spirit will not dwell in a sinful, or wishy washy human. I truly believe that one of the saddest facts about the modern Pentecostal movement is that we can lead people into the gift of tongues and yet they go out the next day and live like the world. The Holy Spirit will not stay in that temple. The gift may remain as it is there, but the Presence is not. That is why some can seemingly walk in the things of the spirit and yet treat other brothers and sister like dirt.

The Holy Spirit is first of all Holy, He is the Spirit of Truth, the Spirit of Love, the comforter and the guide on the inside, but He will not dwell with sin.

1 Peter 1
22 Seeing ye have purified your souls in obeying the truth through the Spirit unto unfeigned love of the brethren, see that ye love one another with a pure heart fervently:23 Being born again, not of corruptible seed, but of incorruptible, by the word of God, which liveth and abideth for ever.

If we make the choice to walk in Love we will walk in the Spirit. That is the whole point behind 1 Corinthians chapters 12 through 14. We can walk in the things of the Spirit for a time without Love but if we walk in Love we will also be walking in the Spirit and all will be made available to us as needed. We are called to choose the right way, the right path, it is narrow and we cannot afford in this hour to just "walk in the spirit", that was allowed for a time to revive the Church but it will not be tolerated from the bride in the last hours. Walking in Love will leads us into the things of the Spirit like Holiness, righteousness, consecration, sanctification etc. We humans will give up anything to get what we Love. We just have not known the standard that was before us that could be obtained.

How we treat others matters because is it tied up in who we are transformed into... Love. If we treat others badly, we cannot and will not grow into the fullness of what is expected. How we treat others matters! The commandment is the key to the fulfillment. He made it that way on purpose and expects us to walk in it. He knows what He is doing.

An Exacting God With An Exacting Word

When I began studying the tabernacle and how it applies to the New Testament believer, I made so many notes and learned so much about how much God Loves us. I had often wondered why He had the writers of the Bible put simple little hints into the Scriptures that for most just seem like part of history or the story. I have since learned over the years that there is nothing written in the Word that was not intended to be there by God. There is a reason for it all and He knew what He was doing. I found that God is an exacting God.

For example, Why did the Gospel writers take the time to record the hour that Jesus was tied to the Cross? Why the noon hour? Why was there darkness for three hours before Jesus actually died? Why did Jesus say "My God, My God why have you forsaken me?" Why did Matthew, Mark, and Luke all record the day in which the transfiguration took place? There is a reason for it all. You see the Word is written for all people, not just one type of person who will believe the simple truth of John 3:16. There are others who need to know the answers to the above questions. He knew exactly what He was doing and He did a great job writing it! The Bible is a long all-encompassing love letter for many different personalities. It all may not mean much to you right now but it all matters to the whole of the body of Christ.

When you study the tabernacle, you can learn how exacting God was in the details and why He had them do things. There was not a single un-purposeful thing in the tabernacle, not any unintentional items in the tents. Everything has a purpose and as it says is Hebrews is a pattern of things to come.

Hebrews 9
23 It was therefore necessary that the patterns of things in the heavens should be purified with these; but the heavenly things themselves with better sacrifices than these. 24 For Christ is not entered into the holy places made with hands, which are the figures of the true; but into heaven itself, now to appear in the presence of God for us:

What was instructed to be done in the earth through Moses was a pattern of things to come, things fulfilled by Jesus.

When we learn that the outer court is built with 66 poles around the court that hang the pure white linen sheets. They are continuous all the way around until you come to the eastern side which has 3 cloth panels of colored cloth. Threads of Red, blue and gold sewn into the cloth gate. This cloth gate represents Jesus, His royalty, His kingship and His Heavenly origin. The gate hangs on 4 posts, representing the 4 gospels. To enter the outer court you must turn your back on the eastern gods and the world and face to the west towards the altar of God. When you enter the outer court, the first thing you see it the brazen altar. This is where the daily sacrificial animals are tied to, hands laid on them and prayers and confessions were made to transfer sin from the person to the sacrifice. On a daily sin confession the person bringing the sacrifice for sin would cut its throat and drain the blood. Parts of the animal were thrown on the fire of the brazen alter. A person could come and make a sacrifice any time or day they wanted, as many times as they wanted. You can come in and out of the outer court as many times as needed to confess and repent for your sins. It always required a stop at the altar. On Passover this was only done once a year by the High Priest for the entire nation. On Passover, the goat was tied to the altar at 9am. At the exact same time Jesus was tied to the Cross.

Passover is one of the feasts that all Jews made the pilgrimage to Jerusalem for. They would all be gathering in the city for days prior to the event. Think about that, millions of extra people in town for this one event that took place every year. Have you ever thought about why the women and kids were on the road with palm leaves when Jesus rode in? Jesus came riding in on a donkey. The crowd was already there. Why did they sing what they sang? Because every year they gathered on that road, for what? To see the two goats being led into the city for the selection of the scape goat and the sacrifice! This time instead Jesus rode in before the goats and the people were inspired to sing to Him! Then before Passover the High Priest would select one of the two goat to be a scape goat to be released and the other to be the blood covering. After the High Priest did this He would go to that laver and wash his hands and say "I am innocent of the blood of this animal" Did not this same thing happen with Jesus and Barabbas! Did not Pilate do the same thing? I have not done the research but I can only imagine what happened to the scape goat, Barabbas!

Let's go back to the outer court, behind the brazen alter, between it and the tent is the laver. This is a large bronze wash bowl that they priests would wash in. We know this as the water baptism. Behind the laver is the tent. I could go in to a lot of details about other items and about the tabernacle but to keep this story moving along I am focusing on the points needed to make the point.

The outer court is not covered, it has high walls of linen that prevent anyone from seeing in or out from ground level but from inside you can still see the sun, moon and stars. You can still gain knowledge from the creation and all of it proclaims the gospel! Knowledge out here is from the brazen alter, (the cross) the laver (water baptism) and the visible things. We can still hear, see, and know from the natural side of things. We still have the light of the sun, moon and stars.

Romans 1
20 For the invisible things of him from the creation of the world are clearly seen, being understood by the things that are made, even his eternal power and Godhead; so that they are without excuse:

Psalm 19
1 The heavens declare the glory of God; and the firmament sheweth his handy work.

It seems that the outer court is the place of a salvation only experience with God. You're forgiven here. You can fall at the altar, the cross as many times as you like, His mercy will always be there. Knowledge is obtained from those in the outer court and the open view of the world. But there is more. This is the Passover experience, the cross. You have your fire insurance. There is more, let's go deeper...

The tent of the Inner court or the Holy place.

The tent is made up of two parts. The only way into either is also from the east side, you cannot enter from any other direction, you must have your back turned on the world, the east. You enter a flap in the inner court on the east side. Inside the only light you see from is from the lamp stand (menorah). It is lit only from fire from the brazen alter. You cannot use any fire you want, you must come by way of the brazen alter. In New Covenant terms we can say that you must have been born again to get this far. The Brazen alter is the cross in New Testament terms, Jesus is the only way! Once inside there is also an incense table which is also only lit by way of the brazen alter. This gives light into the story of Leviticus 10 when Aaron's sons were struck down for trying to use a strange fire to light the fires inside the inner court. There is only one way to God, the cross, only by way of the Cross! Jesus said, I am the way the truth and the life, no one comes to the Father but by way of me! I know it seems like many people are saying that there are many ways to God, but there is not. Jesus is the only way. You must have a cross experience. Today to many so called Christians have a cross less religion and will not enter into the kingdom of God. Only one way.

Once in the inner court, you can also see the showbread table. The showbread is a symbol of the Word of God. It is unleavened. The lamp stand (also call the Menorah) is a symbol of the Holy Spirit. The incense table is a picture of the prayers and worship of the saints. In Acts it says that Cornelius' prayers and acts of worship had come up as a memorial offering to God.

The only light in the inner court comes from the lampstand. You derive knowledge and revelation from the Word and the light of the Spirit. Jesus is the Bread, He is the Word. You need both. Not just Word, not just spirit. Both WORD AND SPIRIT.

This is the place of the Word and the Spirit. We eat of the bread of life daily and drink of the Spirit daily. This place is a symbol of the feast of Pentecost. The place of the baptism of the Holy Spirit. Not just once but continually as Paul said. Acts records that Peter and other of the disciples were filled more than one time.

Acts 2:4
4 And they were all filled with the Holy Ghost, and began to speak with other tongues, as the Spirit gave them utterance.

Act 4
31 And when they had prayed, the place was shaken where they were assembled together; and they were all filled with the Holy Ghost, and they spake the word of God with boldness.

Acts 10
44 While Peter yet spake these words, the Holy Ghost fell on all them which heard the word.

Peter himself was filled three times as recorded in Acts. And we today are satisfied with one and speaking in tongues. I think I would prefer the same as Peter. Fill me Lord, daily!

To enter into the inner court the priests who did so had a higher or we could say a deeper level of consecration to the things of Gods. They had to wash so many times, they had to meet certain conditions and only few priests were able to enter into the inner court. There was a level of consecration and sanctification process that had to be followed. Under the blood this is accomplished as we repent, confess, and then begin to turn away from the things of this world and towards the things of God. The Holy Spirit will guide us away from things of this world and into a deeper walk with Him. You do not just walk into the inner court because you want to. Remember the sons of Aaron that were struck down?

Leviticus 10
1 And Nadab and Abihu, the sons of Aaron, took either of them his censer, and put fire therein, and put incense thereon, and offered strange

fire before the Lord, which he commanded them not. 2 And there went out fire from the Lord, and devoured them, and they died before the Lord.

They attempted to come into the inner court and relight the fire with fire that did not come from the brazen alter. It was a strange fire. It was a fire from another resource not allowed by God. You cannot enter into the inner court without first coming to the cross. Only one way one truth one cross. There are no other ways into the court of God. Before we move on let me make a very important point, the sons of Aaron did not attempt to enter the Holy of Holies, only the inner court. There is no need for fire in the Holy of Holies, fire is only used in the inner court and that coal that lights those fires must come from the brazen alter. They attempted to gain access into the inner court with strange fire and it cost them. You cannot enter into the inner court without first stopping and dealing with sin at the cross. You do not just do what you want to and think it will be accepted by God. He is an exacting God and He has rules. We cannot continue to think He is a grandfather who gives out candy and whatever we want and desire with our denying Him reverence, honor and respect. God is a Holy and exacting God. You must come to Him first under the blood of the lamb. There is a process and a step by step obedience that comes. People want to say that God is a God of grace and you can come just as you are. Yes you can come to the cross just as you are. But once you bow your knee to the Lord, if you truly make Him Lord, you become His. Day by day, every new day you have to give yourself over to Him. You have to submit your free will to His will. That is the beginning of the sanctification process. If you made Him your Lord, you must obey The Lord. There is freedom in that, more than most people think.

The Holy of Holies

When the High Priest entered into the Holy of Holies, well, let's just get a few thing straight about that. One, only one man was ever supposed to be High Priest at a time. Only he never just entered into the Holy of Holies when he wanted. He enter in the Holy of Holies only when allowed by the law. He did not just walk in, he had a long process of preparation and did not just carelessly enter into the room. He was sanctified, consecrated and set apart. He had to be washed 7 times in the laver before being dressed in pure garments. He could not entertain the things of the world and come and go as he pleased. He was not allowed to just say whatever he wanted to say, he could not just wear whatever he wanted. He was as pure and clean and set apart as commanded by God in the law. He was not allowed to participate in the things of the world as others could. The High Priest was not allowed to even mourn the death of a relative.

You see anyone could enter into the outer court as much as they wanted. Then the inner court was for those who has passed through the outer court and consecrated and sanctified to a degree but they did not do whatever they wanted in the inner court. There was a level of holiness and separation that was required. I find it interesting how many people say they are filled with the Holy Spirit yet if they have the Holy Spirit how can they act so unholy? We have forgotten that the Holy Spirit is first of all holy. He does not dwell with those who are in consistent sin and disobedience.

To enter into the Holy of Holies the High Priest had to be sanctified and pure. He could not participate in all the worldly things those residing in the outer court were permitted to do so. The High Priest had to wear certain garments. He was a set apart one for the purpose and plan of God. This is a picture of those today who set themselves apart for the purpose of God, sanctification.

The Holy of Holies is a picture of the feast of tabernacles. All Jewish men were required at this feast. Tabernacle refers to the dwelling place of God. To enter into the Holy of Holies you had to be set apart. When he entered into the Holy Of Holies, He carried the incense from the table in with him. He has eaten of the Shew Bread in the inner court. We have eaten of the Word constantly. He walked in forward and backed out, never turning his back on the Presence of God. The High Priest had to obey the rules set before him. He had to obey! Remember what Jesus said in John 14:23; " if you obey my command, my father and I will take up residence in you!" That comes from obedience. To be consecrated and sanctified, you had to obey! (There is one rule to obey for New Testament believers!) Back to the high priest, who would enter the Holy of Holies at noon. He would stay in there for 3 hours, confessing the sins of the nation before God. Then he would use a hyssop, sprinkle the Mercy Seat with the blood of the sacrifice. Jesus was tied to the cross at nine am, at noon the sky went dark, the same time the High Priest entered into the darkness of the Holy of Holies and it stayed in the dark until the High Priest backed out of the Holy of Holies. It was during this time that the High Priest would transfer the sins of the nation to the blood, and then sprinkle it on the altar. That is when the sin was transferred from the nation to the sacrifice and that is why Jesus said, "My God My God why have you forsaken me." Because God cannot be in the presence of sin. And sin had been transferred to Jesus. God had to turn His back on the sin offering, Jesus. That is why the world went dark for three hours. God turned His back on His son who was the offering of the world. He then died. When the High Priest was doing this the people who gathered into Jerusalem would be in the temple courts. They would gather around the temple singing the psalms from 113 to 120. These were songs sung about the Messiah. While Jesus was hanging on the cross the very people He was sent to die for sang songs about Him.

When the High Priest came out (backing out as he never turned his back on God) of the temple he turned to the people and said "It is finished."

This is why Paul said, He became our high priest

Hebrews 8;1

1 Now of the things which we have spoken this is the sum: We have such a high priest, who is set on the right hand of the throne of the Majesty in the heavens; 2 A minister of the sanctuary, and of the true tabernacle, which the Lord pitched, and not man. 3 For every High Priest is ordained to offer gifts and sacrifices: wherefore it is of necessity that this man have somewhat also to offer. 4 For if he were on earth, he should not be a priest, seeing that there are priests that offer gifts according to the law:5 Who serve unto the example and shadow of heavenly things, as Moses was admonished of God when he was about to make the tabernacle: for, See, saith he, that thou make all things according to the pattern shewed to thee in the mount.

You see God is very exacting and He knew what He was doing. Jesus fulfilled every part of the law and the ceremony of the high priest. He is the High Priest and he has made a way for us. So if he has abolished the need for the ritual of the High Priest and made a way for us, what has He made a way into? Just the outer court, just the inner court? What is different about the inner court that is beyond the baptism of the Holy Spirit? If outer court is salvation, saved by grace, inner court is baptism of the Holy Spirit and the ministry of the Word and the Spirit, what is the Holy of Holies? The Holy of Holies is the tabernacle of God, under the New Testament it is the tabernacle of God with and in us. It is the promise of John 14:23.

In the Holy of Holies there is no fire light, no sound, just darkness, except the Shekinah glory of God. The presence of God between the two cherubim's, on the mercy seat. The only knowledge, light or insight in this room is not derived from seeing or any other of the 5 senses. It is a pure experience with God. It is the intimate place with God and it is the place where you are exposed to your true nature, you are naked before Him. Nothing is hidden, nothing is permitted that is not holy. When you enter into the Holy of Holies, you have no stature, not preeminence, no place in life. You are exposed for all you are. Sin cannot be in the presence of God. He burns it up. The sons of Aaron made a simple but stupid mistake. The men who died touching the ark tried to do the right thing, but died. You do not touch the Holy with the unholy. You do not enter into the presence of God without the blood covering. The High Priest had to cover himself and protect the front of his face with the incense, a barrier between him and the Presence. He needed protection, a covering. Jesus is our High Priest now and he has covered us in the covering of His blood. I refer to this as the rose colored glasses. God sees us through the sinless pure blood of the lamb. Thank God!

Hebrews 4:16

13 Neither is there any creature that is not manifest in his sight: but all things are naked and opened unto the eyes of him with whom we have to do. 14 Seeing then that we have a great high priest, that is passed into the heavens, Jesus the Son of God, let us hold fast our profession. 15 For we have not an High Priest which cannot be touched with the feeling of our infirmities; but was in all points tempted like as we are, yet without sin. 16 Let us therefore come boldly unto the throne of grace that we may obtain mercy, and find grace to help in time of need.

We can come before God now because of that blood covering.

Because Jesus became the High Priest for us, we can come into the presence of God with confidence, to survive for one, but also to have fellowship with our Father. We can interact with Him the way Adam did before the fall. But it does not mean we can come any way we want. We must still come through the cross, we must pass through the laver, we must consecrate to enter into the inner court to be filled and then eat of the Word and learn from the light of the Spirit and pray. We must grow and develop into sanctification and consecration and holiness to enter into the Throne room. Yes we can enter into the throne room, but not without the right preparation. It is not about doing, but it is about the right heart. God is still an exacting God in the New Testament. We must come through Jesus, begin the cleansing; sanctification process, of the Word in our hearts and minds. We must also be consecrated to Him. We can be saved and going to partake of heaven without being in the inner court or Holy of Holies. We must get the things of the world out of our lives and devote ourselves to the Word. In Zac chapter 10 we see that in the latter day (not any later than today) that there will be those who get comfort, vanity, false dreams and visions from a family idol.

Zac 10

1 Ask ye of the Lord rain in the time of the latter rain; so the Lord shall make bright clouds, and give them showers of rain, to every one grass in the field. 2 For the idols have spoken vanity, and the diviners have seen a lie, and have told false dreams; they comfort in vain: therefore they went their way as a flock, they were troubled, because there was no shepherd. 3 Mine anger was kindled against the shepherds, and I punished the goats:

The word used for idol here is used only once in the Word and is refers to a family idol that speaks, but the verse also tells us that the people are seeing something! The family idol that most people bow down to give us ideas, dreams and visions that do not line up with Gods plans and purposes for us. We getting comfort from the wrong source. We cannot be sanctified, holy and consecrated to God if we are bowing down to a family idol that deceives us, lies to us, shows us false dream and speaks to us. God is telling us that there is a day when we will be lead about like lost confused sheep because we bow down to this idol. God goes on to say that His anger is burning against the shepherds who have not spoken against this. We must teach the sheep that the comfort and peace we need is from the Word of God. That is what the very first psalm says! In verse one the prophet lets us know that this will occur in the last days! This goes against the council of God as seen in Psalm 1.

Psalm 1

1 Blessed is the man that walketh not in the counsel of the ungodly, nor standeth in the way of sinners, nor sitteth in the seat of the scornful. 2 But his delight is in the law of the Lord; and in his law doth he meditate day and night. 3 And he shall be like a tree planted by the rivers of water, that bringeth forth his fruit in his season; his leaf also shall not wither; and whatsoever he doeth shall prosper.

I rejoice though as I see in the Word that there is a group that will press into this tabernacle with God. God made a promise that we could and would tabernacle in Him with not a temple made of human hands but by Gods hands. He made us, and when we separate ourselves from the world, we remove every weight and sin that makes us stumble we can enjoy the presence, the majesty of Him tabernacling in us.

That is what Jesus meant when he said in John

John 15

5 I am the vine, ye are the branches: He that abideth in me, and I in him, the same bringeth forth much fruit: for without me ye can do nothing. 6 If a man abide not in me, he is cast forth as a branch, and is withered; and men gather them, and cast them into the fire, and they are burned. 7 If ye abide in me, and my words abide in you, ye shall ask what ye will, and it shall be done unto you. 8 Herein is my Father glorified, that ye bear much fruit; so shall ye be my disciples. 9 As the Father hath loved me, so have I loved you: continue ye in my love. 10 If ye keep my commandments, ye shall abide in my love; even as I have kept my Father's commandments, and abide in his love. 11 These things have I spoken unto you, that my joy might remain in you, and that your joy might be full. 12 This is my commandment, That ye love one another, as I have loved you.

Do you understand that yet? Abide in me, and my Father and I will be in you. How you ask? Well, continue reading. If you obey, obey what? The command of Love. Love that is the word agape and agapao, He uses both here. Practice my love towards God and one another and you will become Love. Abide in my Love and we will live in you! It is about love. This Scripture unlocks it all. It is Love. You want God to tabernacle in you, then abide in His love. Obey His command and in doing so you abide in His love. When you stay hooked up in vital living contact with Love and obey His precepts of Love and the leading of the Spirit of Love, you become that which you've followed after practiced. In doing so God takes up residence in you, He tabernacles in you. No more in the buildings made of man's hand but in God's temples. You and I. So simple and yet so many overlook it. For many, Love is a four letter word that is not worth the study or the actual practice. It is the highest command and yet as a whole we overlook it. Walk in love, abide in Love, become Love and ...

How about this

1 John
3 And hereby we do know that we know him, if we keep his commandments. (his commandment is to love) 4 He that saith, I know him, and keepeth not his commandments, (meaning if you claim to be christ like but do not love) is a liar, and the truth (Love is truth) is not in him. 5 But whoso keepeth his word, in him verily is the love of God perfected: hereby know we that we are in him. 6 He that saith he abideth in him ought himself also to walk, even as he walked. (Paul said "walk in Love)

7 Brethren, I write no new commandment unto you, but an old commandment (walking in love is older than the ten commandments) which ye had from the beginning (that word beginning is the Greek word arche which is referring to the commencement of all things in the beginning of all things!) The old commandment is the word which ye have heard from the beginning. 8 Again, a new commandment I write unto you, which thing is true in him and in you: because the darkness is past, and the true light now shineth. 9 He that saith he is in the light, (just because you call yourself a Christ like one, does not mean you are) and hateth his brother, is in darkness even until now. 10 He that loveth

(love as in the nature of love) his brother abideth in the light, and there is none occasion of stumbling in him.

    Walking in Love as Paul called it is about becoming something different than what we see for the most part today. It is not a religious church thing. It is not just a great way to live, it is the way the truth and the secret to real life. We as Christ-like ones have no other option but to obey, He gave us one command, and we must obey it. Our whole existence, our whole being is tied up in becoming what He has placed in us to become. It is there, stir up the desire to become it. Not just do it, become it. Become Agape, that nature of God in this realm.

    There is something about understanding Agape and Agapao that brings so much into perspective. It will bring Holiness into perspective, it will bring giving into perspective, it will bring fellowship and evangelism into perspective. It bring authority into perspective. We seem to have forgotten our place as a church.

    As a soldier and former Drill instructor, I would have to teach young soldiers how to behave themselves in the presence of a superior officer. You walk on a specific side of the higher ranking officer. You speak only after being addressed. There are many edicts on how to act in the presence of higher rank. It was no different with Jesus and God.

    I asked my sons one day, "Why did Jesus sit at the right hand of the Father?" They could not figure it out. There is a reason and purpose for it. It made the religious leaders very angry and they called it blasphemy but it has to do with equality, something the Pharisees could not grasp. But Jesus did it and in doing so was given a place at God's right hand.

    He sat at the right hand for a reason.

    We must know how to approach God and how to act in His presence. In today's world many people have no etiquette even among other people. In a sense we are all equal but we have lost the respect and honor for our fellow man. We see no value in others, other than what we can get from them. We have no idea what the value of God towards man is and thus we treat each other accordingly. There seems to be no honor, no concern for holy or even honorable things these days. What was once evil is now considered good and God despises that. We do not honor each other, therefore we cannot honor God. It matters to God how we treat others. That is why that is the second command. I love speaking to older men, they have a way about them that demands honor and respect. Most young men today are missing that. Fortunately in many other countries around the world that have not wasted away, honor and respect have priority. God loves us but love as I see it is not like a little kid being spoiled by his grandfather kind of love. That is actually inordinate affection. Ezekiel mentioned this

Ezekiel 33
30 Also, thou son of man, the children of thy people still are talking against thee by the walls and in the doors of the houses, and speak one to another, everyone to his brother, saying, Come, I pray you, and hear what is the word that cometh forth from the Lord. 31 And they come unto thee as the people cometh, and they sit before thee as my people, and they hear thy words, but they will not do them: for with their mouth they shew much love, but their heart goeth after their covetousness. 32 And, lo, thou art unto them as a very lovely song of one that hath a pleasant voice, and can play well on an instrument: for they hear thy words, but they do them not. 33 And when this cometh to pass, (lo, it will come,) then shall they know that a prophet hath been among them.

That word love used in "they show much love" is actually a Hebrew word used only once in the entire bible and it refers to inordinate affection. Fake love. A love that is expressed to get what it wants. Not real love. God see's through it. Much of the church today is described in that verse. We love to hear a good preacher but the proof is in the pudding. Where is the presence of God? It should be with those who love Him. At least that is what Jesus said in John 15 as we quoted earlier. If we obey His command of love, He will make His home in us. He cannot be living in you and not have His presence there. Where He is, the Presence is, where the Presence is, there is power and love. We mock God when we take so lightly the cost of the cross. We mock God when we demand blessing without relationship. We mock God when we abuse His love for us. We mock God in how we treat others apart from His command to love them. We stretch His mercy as far as we can to see what we can get away with and it seems as if the Spirit of God is done stretching for us. He has withdrawn His presence from much of the church and now people run around asking the same thing they asked in Nehemiah's day "Where is the power of God?"

BROTHER JOHN

There is such an attitude of judgment in the church today. I recently had remarked on a post, "it does not make our candle any brighter, blowing out another's candle" Someone replied that that was all Jesus did, to the hypocrites and religious leaders of the day. It is what they said He did in the story of the money changers. Let's think about that. Jesus was the only perfect one. He never stepped out of love. He rebuked those people more because of the way they were treating others! He walked into the gentile court and did not react, he responded. How do I know the difference? Because he had to buy leather, He sat down and spent time braiding that whip. Then after a period of time He responded. He was about love first and judgment last. The mercy of God always proceeds the judgment of God. Jesus Himself said that He did as the Father did, Spoke as He heard the Father speak and saved judgment for Him alone, but if He did make a judgment, He made the right one. I am not saying we should not make decisions or judgments, but when we talk about others, judge others, who we have never prayed with or met. Then make decisions based on rumors and gossip, which includes the twisted mindset of the media, we are in danger. We must cry out to God and seek His will in the matters.

We have so much to grow into, how about we keep our eyes on the road in front of us, instead of looking at all the trash around us. That is how we end up in the ditch not even know it. Keep your eyes on the goal ahead, stay focused on Him. Let's be concerned about our own relationship with Him and not someone else's, who is already in the kingdom. When we do that He will send us to those who do not know Him and then we become effective in fulfilling the mission of the Church. The mission of the Church is honorable and righteousness. It is about others but not condemnation, and reprimanding. You may be disciplined from time to time, but He will handle that. If God can handle you, can He not handle others!

The church is missing something, it is far from the bride of Christ without spot or wrinkle. We must lay down our ways that seem right and run to Him. We must devote ourselves to Him and what He says, not our opinions and attitudes brought in by a sinful nature. Lay it down and lean on Him, seek His wisdom. We have allowed so much of the world's fallen nature into the church and we think that is the way God operates. It is not. We must give up our rights, our judgments, our opinions of others and learn how to see them the way He does. We must learn the truth about compassion, love, and truth. We must learn to dwell in His home -- Not ours that has been whitewashed with seemingly good stuff. Good is not Truth, He is Truth. The tree that we ate of was good, it brought death, and we seem to still be eating of it. We must re learn some things.

God wants us to be in Him, to dwell in His presence, as David said, to hide under the shadow of his wings. He is our strong tower and our buckler. He is, as satan said of Job, A hedge of protection. We must fall down and repent, rise up and begin to obey, very simply, walking, practicing the law of God. Then we can enter into the Holy of Holies. Then we can tabernacle with God.

To enter into the presence of God we can do so boldly and with confidence but not with arrogance and ignorance of Who He is! We must enter with a fear and trembling that humbles us and is thankful for the Blood that allows it. John the revelator fell as if dead at His feet. We will enter His courts with thanksgiving and praise. Not just enter! Not with strange fire. By way of the blood and the name of the one who made a way. Not just because we can. Yes we can but we still must be sanctified and consecrated and approach Him through Jesus and the complete work of Jesus.

I believe that one reason we are not seeing the presence of God and the manifesting of His power in the world today is partly because of our lack of honor, our lack of holiness, our arrogance, our self-righteousness. We may have fire insurance but we also still have self-love. Like Adam after he sinned we still protect our flesh and our way of doing things. We make excuses and blame others for what happens. He still loves us but no man comes to the Father except through Jesus. We have a form of godliness but lack the power there of. I want to explore that tragic situation and God's answer to it in the next section.

Having A Form Of Godliness But Lacking The Power Thereof.

Haggai 2
3 Who is left among you that saw this house in her first glory? and how do ye see it now? is it not in your eyes in comparison of it as nothing?

We hear stories and have read books about men who went before us, and yet when we look for someone today that is doing it and we have to wonder where they are. It seems as if the glory of God skipped a generation. Where is the power of God? Where is the mighty hand of God to perform miracles, signs and wonders? Why do people have to keep dying in sickness? It seems as if since there is such a cry for the things of God yet where are those who will pursue it? In the day of Haggai, he had brought a number of exiles back and they cried when they saw the second temple. It was missing something. Much like then it seems as if the church is missing something.

I find it interesting how many people have become so dissatisfied with the current church model that they turn back to the Mosaic Law to try to satisfy their personal lack and shortcoming. They correctly identify that the Church is without power and missing something but instead of correctly identifying the problem as not with God and His

Word but themselves, they turn to another system or way to try to fill that void. They lack the individual responsibility to change themselves. They are too busy pointing fingers at others and not looking at themselves. As a result they go running after the next new word or revelation. Most of these people mix so much weird stuff with their new Jewish theology that I do not think you can approach each one the same way. I have learned in defending the hearts of others, to keep them from being swayed into this Mosaic Law stuff; is that the real reason they do it, is really a condition of the modern church. The modern church is lacking and they know it, but they try to fill it with something that cannot and never could fill that void.

You cannot fulfill the Mosaic Law. Point blank. Argue it anyway you want there are a number of issues with it but let me address one.

The entire Mosaic Law hinges on the blood sacrifice performed every Passover. If the High Priest does not perform his duties the sin remains. The means that the sin of all Jews has remained since long before Jesus died on the cross.

You may recall that in the Old Testament they were commanded to write the stories down, to share them with their children as they walked on the roads. Think about this, every year 7 times a year all men were required to travel to Jerusalem, on three of those feasts the whole family had to pilgrim to the city. Passover was one of them. Pentecost was required for men only. So as they walked and traveled to the city from wherever they were they would tell the stories of old.

Imagine with me if you would a father and son traveling to Jerusalem for the Day of Atonement feast.

"Hey daddy, why is that holiday called Passover?"

"Well son, this is the day in history that the spirit of death passed over the homes of our ancestors before we were free of Egypt. All the first born were killed that night unless they had the blood painted on the door posts."

"So daddy, why do we sing those songs about a Messiah?"

"Well son, one day He will appear and we will all be saved! We sing about that hope"

"So daddy why do we celebrate Pentecost on this day? And what about Atonement?"

"Well son this feast Pentecost we celebrate, is 50 days after Passover and that is the day Moses came down from Mt Sinai with the presence of God all over him and the law on the tablets. Atonement is the day that the sacrifice is accepted by God and licked up off the Mercy Seat! Son it is an awesome experience, I have heard the stories about your great, great, great grandfather seeing the whirlwind and fire coming down on the Holy of Holies to accept the blood offering."

"Daddy have you seen the fire?"

"No son, I've only heard about it."

"Daddy will we see the fire and wind this year?"

"I hope so son, I hope so..."

Year after year the men would travel to Jerusalem for feasts to obey the requirements of the law. Many young men grew up hearing about the supernatural event that was supposed to have taken place in the past; but, they never actually saw it saw it during their lifetime. Does this sound familiar? Does it feel familiar? Have your heard the stories of old, but not seen them? It seems as if what was once an actual event became history, which became legend which has now become a fairy tale. Do you feel that same familiar emptiness inside when reading that? It feels so similar to today. How many times have you read the Word, only to say to yourself, "Why is there such a difference between the things that happen in the Word and what I see in the real world?" Even the world calls Christianity a fairy tale. Communist Russia has great paintings in large beautiful museums with paintings of Jesus and things Jesus did. They title them "the fairy tale of Jesus doing...." They want you to believe they are fairy tales.

Many a well gifted preacher has been able to turn our attention from the real problem and distracted us from it to the wonderful great life you can have now. But how many times do you hear that and still find yourself empty and wondering. How many times to you have to be led down that blind road of comfort and powerless preaching while there is a path of truth that does exist. Search your heart, you can try to cover the void with reason and knowledge and well thought out arguments, but the void remains. Something is missing.

Use your imagination: Is this how the Jews felt after their returned from exile? Is this how they felt when they returned to the rebuilt temple? They knew that they were God's children but something was missing.

Yet year after year they did what the religious leaders told them to do. Blindly. Why?

Part of it is deception from the enemy but part of it is a deception from the church itself. The High Priest knew the answer. The Levites probably knew the answer but they kept the truth hidden in order to keep up the appearances and keep the lifestyle and authority they thought they had. Sound familiar? Feel familiar?

2 Timothy 3

1 This know also, that in the last days perilous times shall come. 2 For men shall be lovers of their own selves, covetous, boasters, proud, blasphemers, disobedient to parents, unthankful, unholy, 3 Without natural affection, trucebreakers, false accusers, incontinent, fierce, despisers of those that are good, 4 Traitors, heady, highminded, lovers of pleasures more than lovers of God; 5 Having a form of godliness, but denying the power thereof: from such turn away.

Luke 14

35 Behold, your house is left unto you desolate: and verily I say unto you, Ye shall not see me, until the time come when ye shall say, Blessed is he that cometh in the name of the Lord.

Let me share it from another angle.

In Jeremiah we read about the pending judgment that was about to come upon the nation of Israel. Jeremiah was speaking the Word of the Lord that judgment was coming and that they as a nation would be carried away for 70 years. The prophet of God was right. Even as he was speaking the Word of the Lord other ministers were saying "No way! We will have peace and success, Jeremiah is wrong" But His word held true. Before Jerusalem fell and the temple was destroyed the Ark of the Covenant along with all the articles of the Temple were removed and hidden. There is a commonly believed theory about where Jeremiah hid those items but it occurred somewhere around 585-590 BC. Jerusalem fell, many of Israel's young men and women were carried away to Babylon to serve Nebuchadnezzar. A little more than 70 years later Daniel wrote:

Daniel 9:2

2 In the first year of his reign I Daniel understood by books the number of the years, whereof the word of the Lord came to Jeremiah the prophet, that he would accomplish seventy years in the desolations of Jerusalem.

3 And I set my face unto the Lord God, to seek by prayer and supplications, with fasting, and sackcloth, and ashes: 4 And I prayed unto the Lord my God, and made my confession, and said, O Lord, the great and dreadful God, keeping the covenant and mercy to them that love him, and to them that keep his commandments;

So Daniel understood from the Word that the 70 years was over! He found where it was written and did he ignore it? No he began to pray and fast to bring about what he understood should be happening. He understood that according to the Word something was supposed to be happening! Much like today, we can find in the word that something is supposed to happen, but it has not happened yet.

So Daniel began to fast and pray and God raised up Ezra, who rebuilt the temple, Nehemiah who rebuilt the wall, and Haggai who became the voice. Once the temple was done and the wall finished the people began to return to Jerusalem. Haggai records that some people began to cry and wail.

Haggai 2

3 Who is left among you that saw this house in her first glory? and how do ye see it now? is it not in your eyes in comparison of it as nothing?

In Haggai verse 9 of that same chapter it is recorded that the glory of the latter house is supposed to be greater than the former. The former being Solomon's temple which was destroyed prior to the 70 year exile.

The Glory of the latter house is supposed to be greater than the glory of the former, but in this instance those who had seen the first temple, Solomon's temple, knew something was missing. This new temple was nothing in comparison to Solomon's. There was no Glory on it. They had seen the temple as kids and knew something was missing. What was it? The presence of God was missing and they knew it.

The Glory did not reside on the Temple or even within the second Temple. It resided on the Mercy Seat on the Ark of Covenant, which was placed in the Holy of Holies. The Temple is the house but the Glory came because of the Ark. The Ark of the Covenant was the thing that carried the presence of God. The Shekinah Glory of God resided between the cherubim on the mercy seat. Have you ever met someone who just seemed to be covered in the presence of God? They had the presence and your heart knew it. You knew it down on the inside. It was refreshing it was wonderful. Then think about people who you've met who stated that they were Christians but something was off... something just seemed to be missing.

One way to explain this knowing of the Spirit is with Jude.

Jude 12

12 These are spots in your feasts of charity, when they feast with you, feeding themselves without fear: clouds they are without water, carried about of winds; trees whose fruit withereth, without fruit, twice dead, plucked up by the roots;

Jude is referring to men and he compares them to rainless, clouds. A cloud should bring rain and a refreshing cool wind. You expect a time of refreshing from a cloud. When you see a fruit tree you expect fruit that is why Jesus cursed that fruit tree from the roots. In comparison we are supposed to be like trees planted by rivers of water, not fruitless dry trees. Clouds bring a time of refreshing, rain, and a cool breeze. But these men who sneak in to the congregations have nothing refreshing about them. Something is missing. Down on the inside you know this.

Let's look at Zechariah 10;1

Zechariah 10;1

1 Ask ye of the Lord rain in the time of the latter rain; so the Lord shall make bright clouds, and give them showers of rain, to every one grass in the field.

In this passage we see that clouds are a good thing. We can see in this Scripture that like Daniel we can ask for something because we have a time frame here: In the time of the latter rain. Would not the time of the latter rain be the same as the last rain? The last day! We can see from this and other Scriptures that in the last day, there would be an outpouring of rain. This is the last day! No day after this current one for men in this era! He says, "Ask Ye" so we like Daniel have to ask. Then when we do, He will give us bright clouds. So does that mean that he will give us clouds that will float around causing miracles and wonders? No, and He will not be riding in a cloud like Zeus throwing lightning bolts at people, "You're healed, Boom! You're saved Boom!" No He will raise up clouds, men who will be like refreshing clouds full of rain and something else. Bright. I like that word as it is used only once in the entire Bible in Hebrew and it refers to lightening. So God will raise up men with the lightening of God and showers of rain. I see that this is a Scripture that refers to men and women in the last days who will be full of the Spirit, overflowing with rivers of flowing water, who will see miracles, signs, and wonders! But these men and women are refreshing. Not dry rainless clouds. There is a difference and most of us can identify it if we will take the time and examine the Word.

When I first met my wife, we would go out to eat, sometimes that restaurant food was not very tasty. Instead of complaining about that restaurant for the next 30 minutes I would just say, "I do not have to eat there again." I do that same thing with preachers. If the Word is off, if the Spirit is not present, I do not speak ill about the child of God. I simply say "I do not need to eat there again" There is no need to speak ill about someone. I can pray and hope God will bless the preacher. Just move on and don't eat there again.

If there is no presence on a preacher or a church as there was not on the second temple, don't eat there again. The problem is and just the same as it was in the days of Jesus, the religious leaders need and want that attention and distract the people from the real problem, no presence, to keep us from eating good food.

Let go back to what I mentioned earlier, When the Jews came back to Jerusalem and saw the temple, they knew something was missing, the presence of God, the Glory. There was no ark in the temple. It has yet to be returned. If there is no ark there is no altar and there is no presence of God. As I often get into conversations with people who want others to submit to Mosaic Law and so often I ask them. How can you obey that law if there is not an altar to sprinkle the blood on? You see there was not another altar given to sprinkle the blood on. There was no ark in the temple in the days of Jesus, so the High Priest had to know this as he went into the Holy of Holies once a year. He was defrauding the people. Making them do all the religious duty and customs but to no avail. But the people did not know this. They were distracted by the lies of the high priest. How could you demand the people obey the law when there was no way to satisfy the law since there was not an altar to sprinkle the blood on? That is why the day of the sacrifice being accepted and being licked off the altar by fire and wind coming down was now a legend or even a fairy tale. The modern church is in the same position now. Much of what we have been told and taught seems like a fairy tale.

    The Jewish men of every nation were gathered together in Jerusalem for the required feast they hoped and longed for the fire and smoke to descend and lick up the blood sacrifice left on the altar. They had heard the story over and over. They shared it with each other and taught it to their children as they walked along the streets to pilgrim back for the feast. But it had not happened since sometime around 585 BC. Without the mercy seat being present, there was no completion to the blood sacrifice; therefore there was no need for the fire and wind of God to lick up the blood off the mercy seat. They did not send a maid into the Holy of Holies to clean up the blood the day after the sacrifice. No! God accepted it with tongues of fire and a whirlwind. The same fire, smoke, and wind that led them by day and night in the desert, settled on the Temple and it appeared to demonstrate to the whole nation, to all those present that the sacrifice had been accepted by God! But sadly is was a legend by the days of Jesus. It's a fairy tale now.

    Think about this. Often I have heard that the reason the curtain to the Holy of Holies was rent and fell from top to bottom was to allow or signify that the presence of God had left the Temple. But how could that have been if there was not an Ark of the Covenant in the Holy of Holies? There was no Shekinah Glory in the Holy of Holies of the second temple. The other reason the curtain fell and split was to expose the lie! We can assume that only the High Priest knew that the Holy of Holies was empty and when the curtain ripped it exposed the lie. Everyone who was present for the feast and in the temple, now knew the lie! (just a side note, there were two priests at the time of Jesus, which was against the law, also the whole thing taught about the rope tied to the priest to go into the holy of holies, only occurred during the period after the 2nd temple was built.

They could get away with it then as there was no presence in the temple then. Prior to the exile there was no way they could have gotten away with those scams!)

Many of us know that something is wrong, men parade around running their mouths about having the power of God. Many make a lot of money making these proclamations. Like the priests of the temple, they know they lack the power the presence but nice words and well sounding sermons have deceived the people. Few if any are walking in the presence and therefore the Presence and the Glory have become stuff of legend and even fairy tales. The world laughs at us because as a Church we have people manifesting stuff but not Him. They can tell that something is wrong but we as a church continue to run after the false and fine sounding doctrine but they are not in pursuit of the presence of God.

.

We must be willing to obey in any manner He wants personally, to enter into the Holy of Holies. The world and the church are crying out for it. I believe it will take men and women who will turn their backs on the things of the world and cry out like John the Baptist, even at the sake of our own ministries and desires.

I must decrease and He must increase. I would add, at all cost!

Infallible Proofs

ACTS 1:3
3 To whom also he shewed himself alive after his passion by many infallible proofs, being seen of them forty days, and speaking of the things pertaining to the kingdom of God:

I am convinced that the thing all men look for and will silence the critics and the frauds is simply the infallible proofs of the resurrection of Jesus. I do not hold to the doctrine that many do that the proof of the Baptism of the Holy Spirit is tongues. I believe that those who are truly baptized in the Holy Spirit will speak in tongues but it is not the proof. I see over and over that the proof of the Holy Spirit in the believer is power. The infallible proofs. Not generally calling out of healings that really never manifest, not stories about a healing that took place in this town, but there was no camera or other witnesses. I believe from everything I read in the Word that when a man or women gets filled with the Holy Spirit that there will be power and Infallible proofs. Otherwise Jesus is a liar. In His own words

Acts 1:8
8 But ye shall receive power, after that the Holy Ghost is come upon you; and ye shall be witnesses unto me both in Jerusalem, and in all Judaea, and in Samaria, and unto the uttermost part of the earth.

Jesus is quoted here, "and you shall receive Power." Power point blank. Power is not limited to speaking in tongues, I see a great place for the manifest gift of speaking in tongues but that is not the proof of the Baptism of the Holy Spirit according to Jesus. Even in the Gospels, after Jesus was baptized in the Spirit and then the consecration of the 40 day fast in the wilderness, it says, He returned in Power. There is not one recorded instance of Jesus speaking in tongues. I am not in any way denying tongues and that gift but when we have made it the gold standard of the Holy Spirit dwelling in man, but denied the complete working of the Holy Spirit to produce Holiness in us...something is off. How can we say we have the Holy Spirit and yet live like animals, in sin, back biting, gossiping? Gossip alone is one of the things God hates, and yet how many self-proclaimed Spirit filled believers thrive in gossip? How can Holiness and un-holiness live in the same house? Something is off.

    I struggled with speaking in tongues for a while and God Himself proved it to me. I was in prayer one night at a prayer meeting under a table hiding from others. As I prayed in the Spirit I heard the language change to what sounded like something oriental. At that same moment I saw a women who had a round face, black hair and brown skin saying to me, "Come here to us." Well I recorded it in the journal of that church as this was part of a 24 hour prayer program that I was part of. A few week later I met a man who was from a closed nation and just after speaking to him I said "I hope someday I get to go to ..." I had never even heard of that nation. Well about a year later after many times praying in two different languages in the Spirit; one being this new oriental langue, I found myself in India. I was traveling up into Nepal and Bhutan to recruit students for Bible School in Calcutta and to help graduates start their churches. I went through a long and at the time unknown interrogation, by some underground church pastors in Bhutan. I had no idea these men were pastors and they did not reveal it to me until they trusted me. After an all-day visitation, still not knowing anything other than what felt like a wasted day, they revealed who they were and invited me to go into Bhutan. I ended up being so blessed and then even went into a refugee camp under protection of the UN in Nepal and ministered to many Bhutanese refugees. This was a wonderful experience. I could go into details about miracles God did and protection as well, but my point here is about tongues. After getting to go into these places that were very much a legal no no, I ended up back in India and in a bible school along the border of Bhutan. I was asked to minister in the school and prior to doing so I went into a room with several people and we began to pray. After several minutes, that new language came out and I kept praying,

(I am not a loud prayer) and the room grew quiet. I stopped praying and looked at my friend and asked "What's wrong?" Someone spoke up and he looked at me and said, "They say you speak beautiful Dzongkha" (jo uc ka) "Dzongka I asked?" "Yes, you speak a beautiful but old form of Dzongkha." The language of Bhutan. They told me that I was giving some of the most awesome praise and honor to God imaginable! I never had any idea! At that same moment I looked across the room and saw the young lady I had seen in the prayer room when I began to pray in that language! Since that time I have not prayed in that tongue again that I am aware of.

Jude 1
20 But ye, beloved, building up yourselves on your most holy faith, praying in the Holy Ghost, 21 keep yourselves in the love of God, looking for the mercy of our Lord Jesus Christ unto eternal life.

Please notice here that the two verses are one complete sentence. We must stay in the love of God. It is not just about gifts and "supernatural" things, it is first about love. Jude was reminding them to stay where they were already living, in love! Stay in Love, build yourself up in your holy faith by praying in the Spirit. Entire sects of the church have built themselves a teaching and doctrine that relies on the gift of tongues. It is not meant to be but has become a "symbol" of holiness with them. Unfortunately that would mean that Hindus, Muslims and witch doctors around the world are holy as well, Christians are not the only ones who pray in tongues. The devil has fakes everywhere. I recently heard of a Hindu priest claiming he was doing miracles by the Holy Ghost, because he spoke in tongues.

God proved to me that tongues is real but I cannot find in the Word that it is the only sign of the baptism of the Holy Spirit. The other gifts are gifts too. They too are symptoms of the Holy Spirit. No one gift is the only gift or symptom. Power and infallible proofs are the proof. Having the holiness of God should be part as well. And if God is Love and God is the Holy Spirit, then Love and holiness should be proof as well. Jesus Himself stated in

John 13:34

A new commandment I give unto you, That ye love one another; as I have loved you, that ye also love one another. 35 By this shall all men know that ye are my disciples, if ye have love one to another.

Love would be the reason others would know we are His disciples. I am convinced that most people who think they are filled with the Holy Spirit are not. Tongues can be taught and with a little deception it can be a learned experience, but without the holiness, the love and the infallible proofs, all we do is produce a weak and powerless church that eventually creates critics and combatants to what we are trying to build. Those people who have been duped or tricked into the powerless baptism will figure it out. Most of the time they are not as happy as it appears. What will be the excuse when the power and infallible proofs of God's love for us in miracles, signs and wonders do come on the scene? What excuse will be made by those who have not the real Holy Spirit?

I have a problem and that is I do not like fakes. I do not like liars. I want as many people as possible to be filled with the real power of God and not conned into a fake spiritual experience that just adds to the low level of spirituality that the Church already has. We have forgotten the ancient ways and the paths of righteousness and holiness.

Jeremiah 6:16

16 Thus saith the Lord, Stand ye in the ways, and see, and ask for the old paths, where is the good way, and walk therein, and ye shall find rest for your souls. But they said, We will not walk therein.

There is a path to holiness, righteousness and power that is not being sought or taught. An ancient path -- Enoch walked in that path. Noah walked in that path. Abraham walked in it too. It is an old path – an ancient path. How many times do we have to see loved ones die, dragging them from preacher to preacher and church to church in search of the real power, exhausting our finances and energy looking for the Presence, only to see our loved ones die? When will we get so exhausted with ourselves and the games we have been tricked into playing and wake up? We cannot blame preachers, we cannot blame the Church. There is nothing wrong with God. There is nothing wrong with the Word. The problem has to be in what we are doing. We are the problem. We have to admit it is us. We must accept responsibility for the shortcomings we cause in our own lives.

We have bought into the modern church program of atmosphere verses Presence. We have a form of godliness but no power. Admit it, then begin to search for the ancient path as Jeremiah stated. If it was ancient in Jeremiahs day, how ancient is it now?

Recently in class I began just in the book of Acts going through with the students and highlighting every supernatural thing that took place. I then went through the Gospels, then the Old Testament. Have you ever taken the time to look at how supernatural this thing called Christianity is? My goodness, the entire thing from Genesis to Revelation is supernatural! It is so full of miracle signs and wonders! What has happened to the human race that we no longer see that? I know the answer but my goodness, think about that for a few minutes. Pick up a color pencil and go to Acts 1 and begin reading, you will color every column and every page multiple times. This whole thing we say we believe is full of supernatural events. I cannot find one hint anywhere that says it stopped. I think like the Jews from 585- 590 BC to present day, it has become a legend and fairy tale because the people who have risen to the top have been fleecing us. We accepted a lower standard of relationship with God, a lower standard of Christianity and a lower standard of love. We make up well sounding arguments to back up our lack and our godlessness. We can argue for hours the reasons that justify our lack of The Presence. I have learned that the further a man gets from the original intent of what God intended him to be the more "theological" he has to get.

I hear a voice rising from around the world. There is a unified cry coming up as the awakening begins, people are voicing their frustration and like the people returning to the City and seeing the new temple, they are crying out "Foul!" People are recognizing that there is something missing, where is the promised Glory?

It is time to repent, it is time to rend our hearts, it is time to not accept the false and the plaudit seekers, it is time to fast, cry and lament before a Holy God. It is time to use the faith we have been taught to use to bring about the greatest outpouring of His Presence and the Harvest.

Miracles, signs and wonders are the dinner bell to the Gospel, not a get quick rich scheme. The days of Ananias and Sapphira are upon us and you will see many fall before their time. Please check your heart and keep it pure and pursue His love so that as this outpouring begins you can participate and help reap the Harvest. Get rooted in grounded and stay there. Don't let anything get you out of your Love connection with Him.

Remember the Holy Spirit is the Spirit of Love, He is the Spirit of Holiness as well. We cannot allow Him to fill us and let it all leak out because we cannot remain consecrated or sanctified. Be ye Holy as He is Holy! Be Love as He is Love.

Where are the mighty men of Valor? I believe most are not behind the pulpits of the United States. They cannot be found in the halls of congress or the courts. They are hidden from view for now but they are about to rise up in light and power and they will be marked with something that most have not seen. (Rev 9:4) The nature of Love will exude from and to others. It will heal and transform, it will bind up the broken heart, release the oppressed and declare the end is near. They will probably not have Bible school degrees, college transcripts or even be ordained into the ministry. Jesus was not. He will be there example and teacher.

Luke 4
18 The Spirit of the Lord is upon me, because he hath anointed me to preach the gospel to the poor; he hath sent me to heal the brokenhearted, to preach deliverance to the captives, and recovering of sight to the blind, to set at liberty them that are bruised, 19 To preach the acceptable year of the Lord. 20 And he closed the book, and he gave it again to the minister, and sat down. And the eyes of all them that were in the synagogue were fastened on him. 21 And he began to say unto them, This day is this scripture fulfilled in your ears.

Where are the mighty men of Valor? Here Am I Lord. Let me taste of the death and the power of the resurrection! You don't need to tie a rope around your ankle to make it seem like you have the Presence, the people will know. We live in a day of infallible proofs and the genuine will expose the false and dross.

Transformed

I recently did a word study on this word Transformed. There are two different words we can study.

Romans 12:1
1 I beseech you therefore, brethren, by the mercies of God, that ye present your bodies a living sacrifice, holy, acceptable unto God, which is your reasonable service. 2 And be not conformed to this world: but be ye transformed by the renewing of your mind, that ye may prove what is that good, and acceptable, and perfect, will of God.

This word transformed in the Strong's concordance is the word metamorphoo, you may recognize it as it is very similar to the word we use, metamorphosis. It means to be transfigured, changed into, and to be transformed. From one thing into another. It is much like a caterpillar that goes into a cocoon and comes out a different thing altogether. We are to be the same way. God puts a deposit of His nature in us. He expects us to grow that deposit into the thing He made us to be born again into.

Romans 5:5
5 And hope maketh not ashamed; because the love of God is shed abroad in our hearts by the Holy Ghost which is given unto us.

God made a deposit in us, He expects us to grow into it. The blue print was placed in us and we have the instructions to becoming what He wants written on our hearts. We are supposed to be transformed into, changed into something, and transfigured into something.

The blueprint is there, we need to follow it. It is not to be a Christian, but to become a Christ like one. We are born again to become, grow into, and mature into something that we are not. We must progress into what He wants us to be. It is not just about salvation in the sense of staying out of hell or getting into heaven. He wants us to grow into something spiritual in the earthly realm. Jesus was the first born of many sons, not the only one. We are sons of God too.

Adam was created to fellowship with God. He was a spirit that possessed a body. He was led, controlled by the spiritual man he was created to be. He was created in the image of God. Now get this, God is a Spirit, right? John also tells us that God is Love. The nature of Love, the being of love. Not just a God who acts in love but He is Love. It is a noun. He is the Spirit of Love. That same Spirit is what was brooding over the earth. When God created Adam, He created him In His image. The Image of Love! The image of Agape! Adam was a love creature, until he chose to sin. Then He was born again into the physical realm. Sin set in and death became the end. Jesus came under the terms of the physical sin fallen world and was born into sin and death like every man. But He was the first born of the Spirit. He provided a way out of the sin physical world and into the born again spiritual realm. He was the way the path the life for a reason. He walked the way and on the path we are to walk on. He was transformed in the inner man to become what He and God had intended all along. He showed us the way to live within the realm of God. The realm of God, the realm of Love. Jesus was the manifest expression of who God is. Love. He then commanded us to walk in love, saying it has been the law that was from the beginning. The law of Love is the law of the Spirit. We were born into a fallen sin world. We have been given a path out, and ancient path called love. Find the ancient path and walk in it. It existed before Abraham, Moses and even Adam. It is Love.

Jesus was our shining example of love and He showed us the way. Love is the basis of the beginning and it will be all there is in the end. Not the love of each other, that allows us to expect things, expect certain treatment but Love that is defined primarily in its forgiveness and giving.

John 3

16 For God so loved the world, that he gave his only begotten Son, that whosoever believeth in him should not perish, but have everlasting life. 17 For God sent not his Son into the world to condemn the world; but that the world through him might be saved.

God so loved, which is also His nature, that He gave Jesus to forgive us. God created us, loved us, and provided the lamb to save us. If we let him, He will cause growth in us that only He can bring about. We must pursue as Paul said, the most excellent way, Love. We are born again to become not just Christians and church goers, or get out of hell and into heaven goers, but Love. We are to become love. We become the greatest expression of His love in this earth. Re born out of a sin nature and back in to the Love nature that Adam gave up. We were created by Love for Love. It is the nature of the born again child of God. We are to act like our dad of love.

When we allow ourselves to fall so in love with God that we begin to act like Him, as it says in

Ephesian 5
1 Be ye therefore followers of God, as dear children; 2 And walk in love, as Christ also hath loved us, and hath given himself for us an offering and a sacrifice to God for a sweet smelling savour.

Most translations use the word imitators. That word in the Greek is mimetes, it is where we get the English word, mimic. We must imitate God. In doing so we will primarily give and forgive. It brings us to the point we made elsewhere that as we imitate God the Father, we as His children begin to act like Him. As we act like Him we soon begin to develop habits that lead to a habitation.

2 Peter 1
4 Whereby are given unto us exceeding great and precious promises: that by these ye might be partakers of the divine nature, having escaped the corruption that is in the world through lust.

I want to escape the pattern and corruption of the fallen world. To do so we must be partakers of the divine nature. That word partaker is the Greek word Koinonos, which refers to partner in equal value or fellowship. Think of that, Peter is telling us that if we become partakers of the divine nature we will escape the nature of the fallen world. What is the nature of God? It is love. Agape love, the noun. As we agapao, or practice the law that has existed since the beginning we begin to be transformed into a new creature, a new creation, one that world has been searchING. We become like our father, we act like our father, we love like our father. We become the expression of love in this world.

Let's take a look at another word very similar but a little different.

2 Cor 12
14 And no marvel; for Satan himself is transformed into an angel of light. 15 Therefore it is no great thing if his ministers also be transformed as the ministers of righteousness; whose end shall be according to their works.

This word transformed is the Greek word metascharatizo. It translates into the same English word but it has a negative meaning. It refers to the putting on of a disguise. Much like someone who wants to not be seen for who they really are and hide themselves, this is that type of meaning. It is not used in any sense of the word for those who are to be transformed into the children of God. It is a negative word that speaks of hiding something, not becoming something new.

I also want to take a moment to raise your prophetic timing antenna. I am a firm believer that everything in the Word of God is there for a reason. The best interpretation of Scripture is Scripture. If you take the time to study you will find the answers in the Word. I personally enjoy the truth that portions of the Bible were written thousands of years apart and yet they fit together like a wonderful puzzle. You can often find the key to unlock an Old Testament prophecy in the New Testament or vice versa.

Here is a little nugget to study. In speaking of being transformed one of the definitions is the word transfigured. Jesus was transfigured and His spiritual being overtook His physical being. What was on the inside, once shut up like fire in Jeremiah's bones, and now became visible on the outside of the physical man. The real Jesus was revealed. Now this often is overlooked wording from each account of the mount of transfiguration.

Matthew 17
1 And after six days Jesus taketh Peter, James, and John his brother, and bringeth them up into an high mountain apart, 2 And was transfigured before them: and his face did shine as the sun, and his raiment was white as the light.

Mark 9

And after six days Jesus taketh with him Peter, and James, and John, and leadeth them up into an high mountain apart by themselves: and he was transfigured before them.

Luke 9

28 And it came to pass about an eight days after these sayings, he took Peter and John and James, and went up into a mountain to pray. 29 And as he prayed, the fashion of his countenance was altered, and his raiment was white and glistering.

Frist let me point out that the word transfigured here in Matthew and Mark are the same transfigured that Paul used in our earlier discussion about us being transformed. In the Greek they are the same word. Him and then us, if we will let Him.

Also look at the timing of all three Gospel accounts. After six days, before the eighth day. All point to one day, the seventh. Some versions say that about the seventh day in Mark. The point being the day it is referring to is the seventh day. We just moved into the seventh day since Adam. We crossed into the seventh day after the year 2000. I don't believe in coincidence in the Word of God.

Recall what Hosea said,

Hosea 6

After two days will he revive us: in the third day he will raise us up, and we shall live in his sight. 3 Then shall we know, if we follow on to know the Lord: his going forth is prepared as the morning; and he shall come unto us as the rain, as the latter and former rain unto the earth.

In the third day we will tabernacle with Him. Some have said that would take place after we were taken to heaven, if so then that would render verse 3 obsolete, there would be no need for "latter and former rain"

I could go further but suggest you read, Why are the Fishermen Eating the Bait? to get more specific details and in depth study of that.

The point being we are to be transformed, from one nature into another. We are to become partakers of the nature of God that has been shed abroad in our heart. The pattern is there, we need to follow it.

The pattern of the nature of God was shed aborad in our hearts when we accept Jesus as our Lord. While we were yet sinners, God demonstrated His love for us, sending Jesus and given to us a portion of His nature; a talent you could say, that we are responsible for growing. We can die a baby child of God or we can become mature and obtain the fullness of God, by growing in Love. We are not called to just be saved from Hell and into Heaven. We are called and recreated to become the children, the imitators, the mimickers of God -- To be like Him in this realm. The blueprint was put in us when we were born again.

Romans 5:5
5 And hope maketh not ashamed; because the love of God is shed abroad in our hearts by the Holy Ghost which is given unto us.

The reason most people have controversy with God is that they deny the nature that is in them, put there by God, love. They refuse to walk according to the new nature that was recreated in them. They are therefore at odds with themselves, or at least the nature that was put in them. They have not been told or learned that they are now suppose to be creatures of love. Instead they are accepted as those who have confessed and still act as if they did before, like the fallen nature they were born into. They do not know that they are out of sync with their true nature of love. Then they also look up from what they read in their Bibles and see something different than what they just read and they doubt what they read. Or they are told that they misconstrued or just do not understand the Bible. Therefore they are not following the path written on their hearts. Therefore God holds back His presence and His promises. Maybe we need to quit understanding with our eyes.

Let examine another Scripture

Colossians 3
10 And have put on the new man, which is renewed in knowledge after the image of him that created him:11 Where there is neither Greek nor Jew, circumcision nor uncircumcision, Barbarian, Scythian, bond nor free: but Christ is all, and in all.12 Put on therefore, as the elect of God, holy and beloved, bowels of mercies, kindness, humbleness of

mind, meekness, longsuffering; 13 Forbearing one another, and forgiving one another, if any man have a quarrel against any: even as Christ forgave you, so also do ye. 14 And above all these things put on charity, which is the bond of perfectness.

In the original Greek the word eikon is used which means a pattern or original image. Verse 10 could read like this

10 And have put on the new man, which is renewed in knowledge after the original pattern of Him that created him:

Verse 10 tells us that that man was originally another way! We need to find that original pattern and walk in it. He gives us a hint as he progresses in the chapter as he describes the character traits of love and then finally tells us to put on Agape! Put on the nature of God. Put on the spirit of who you were originally created to be! Adam was created in the image of love and so are we who have been born again -- act like it! Begin to practice Agapao on a daily basis and put on the nature of Agape! The confusion so many walk in is because they refuse to or do not know that they are supposed to walk according to the nature that was deposited in them. Therefore they have a disconnect inside, something seems off. They search for it in the media, in books, in whatever but they are not finding it. They are not at peace because there is controversy in their lives. They have a pattern on the inside but walk according to the world on the outside. Therefore since they are not in vital living contact with the Father and the branch on the inside they do not live off the sap that flows from the vine. They are out of touch and with the nature they want to be and have inside but they are trying to do it according to the worlds methods which have overrun most of the church. We live in the time of the latter and the last rain and harvest is coming but we do not see the rain. We are to blame, not God. If I were to ask a fruit tree to make peanuts, well we would have a problem. If we teach people to continue to act like the world, well we do have a problem. We are supposed to act like the seed that was sown in us. We are to act like the Love that was shed abroad in our hearts. We are to act like our Father, Love.

Jer 5

24 Neither say they in their heart, Let us now fear the Lord our God that giveth rain, both the former and the latter, in his season: he reserveth

unto us the appointed weeks of the harvest. 25 Your iniquities have turned away these things, and your sins have with holden good things from you.

In

In The Beginning

Romans 8
1 There is therefore now no condemnation to them which are in Christ Jesus, who walk not after the flesh, but after the Spirit. 2 For the law of the Spirit of life in Christ Jesus hath made me free from the law of sin and death. 3 For what the law could not do, in that it was weak through the flesh, God sending his own Son in the likeness of sinful flesh, and for sin, condemned sin in the flesh:4 That the righteousness of the law might be fulfilled in us, who walk not after the flesh, but after the Spirit.

We have been set free from the law of sin and death. Many today want others to submit themselves to part or portions they have decided are worthy of following, but Paul tells us we are free. The law of sin and death could never make us what we desired to be. No one was able to walk in it fully other than Jesus. We are free from the law of sin, and free to follow the law of Christ, the law of the Spirit, which is the law of Love. To be free to follow the law of love is a higher standard but it brings with it a higher reward. It brings within it the ability to transform us into what He wants us to be. It will seem too many to be a law that has no rules but once you begin to walk in it you will find it is the highest possible law there is. It is not easy for the flesh to submit to the law of the Spirit, but by the Spirit leading and the grace of Jesus we can do it day by day. In the long run we become something like what the world has not currently seen. We transform into something different than what the world is offering. We become the sons and daughters of God. Love is strong enough to do it. I could not have walked the road to the crucifixion and not given up. I could not have walked out being spit on and mocked and knowing that I was innocent. Jesus could and He gives us the same Spirit He had. He allowed it to transform Him into what God wanted and He obeyed to the end. We don't have to do what Jesus did in His death but we are supposed to become like Him in our life.

Let's go to the beginning

Isaiah 46

10 Declaring the end from the beginning, and from ancient times the things that are not yet done, saying, My counsel shall stand, and I will do all my pleasure:

In the beginning God created man and in the image of man He created us. We once knew what the image of God was, but we gave it up through Adam's sin, but God made a way and knew a way from the beginning that is ancient and older than man himself. God was and always will be. Man was not but can be.

1 John 1

1 That which was from the beginning, which we have heard, which we have seen with our eyes, which we have looked upon, and our hands have handled, of the Word of life; 2 (For the life was manifested, and we have seen it, and bear witness, and shew unto you that eternal life, which was with the Father, and was manifested unto us;)

John 1

1 In the beginning was the Word, and the Word was with God, and the Word was God. 2 The same was in the beginning with God. 3 All things were made by him; and without him was not anything made that was made.

Matthew 22

36 Master, which is the great commandment in the law? 37 Jesus said unto him, Thou shalt love the Lord thy God with all thy heart, and with all thy soul, and with all thy mind. 38 This is the first and great commandment. 39 And the second is like unto it, Thou shalt love thy neighbour as thyself. 40 On these two commandments hang all the law and the prophets.

I share these verses to begin this chapter as they have some common words. In the Greek the word beginning is Arche, meaning, at the commencement of all things, one version of the Bible uses the phrase, "that has always existed" instead of the word beginning. So the Word and God have always existed, always been. Jesus then in Matthew 22 when being questioned by a lawyer says of the law of Love, is has been from the beginning, He said, this is the first and last commandment. This word for first comes from the same root of the word beginning. The law of love existed prior to man, prior to Abraham, prior to Moses and it will continue forever. The law of love has and will always be. God is love and that word used to describe God as love is Agape. Agape is God, and it has always existed. Always will.

Other verses that use that same word in the Greek, Arche are

Mark 10:6
 But from the beginning of the creation God made them male and female.

1 john 2:7
Brethren, I write no new commandment unto you, but an old commandment which ye had from the beginning. The old commandment is the word which ye have heard from the beginning.

Jesus is telling them that this is the original command, it always was and always will be. To walk in Agapao

1John 2:24
Let that therefore abide in you, which ye have heard from the beginning. If that which ye have heard from the beginning shall remain in you, ye also shall continue in the Son, and in the Father.

From the beginning again is that word Arche, it was heard in the beginning long before the Mosaic law was handed down.

2 John 5-6
And now I beseech thee, lady, not as though I wrote a new commandment unto thee, but that which we had from the beginning, that we love one another. 6 And this is love, that we walk after his

commandments. This is the commandment, that, as ye have heard from the beginning, ye should walk in it.

John is making it very clear here: From the very first of all things as we know them, there has been a law that always existed. Stay in obedience to that command. The law of love that has been and always will be is what Able walked in, Enoch walked in, Noah walked in, Abraham walked in, so forth and so on. Love was and always will be the greatest command.

Rev 22:13 I am Alpha and Omega, the beginning and the end, the first and the last.

Love has been from times eternal until times eternal. It is as wide as it is high. It is as deep as it is long. We are told that God removed our sin from us as far as the east is from the west. You know what He put in its place? His love for us. As far as wide can be, as high as high can be, as deep as deep can be. You will never reach the end of the love of God no matter what direction you go. That is why Paul tells us to be rooted and grounded in love, and we will no longer be infants swayed back and forth by the cunning teachings of men, but becoming mature into the fullness of Christ. Christ is the fullness of love! This is not just the emotion or feeling of love but the Nature, the person of love!

Love is eternal both forward and backward in time. It always was and always will be! It is what we will be doing in heaven! For eternity!

Most people think of Love as a character trait. A virtue that you can use as needed. Many people think that you can step in and out as needed and that loving others will help you get what you need. That action is what we would call Phileo Love. It is generated in the soul and mind of man. It is calculated. I actuality think alot of the church walks in inordinate affection. They care more about feelings and what others think than they do the truth. They care about the love, affection, and approval of men more than the truth. You cannot separate love from truth. Jesus said He was the truth and God is love, and they are one.

The love of God is not just something you walk in as Paul said "Let's walk in Love." You must first be born again, God deposits a portion of His love in you and you must do something with it. Think of the parable of the talents. God has placed a talent of His love, His nature in you. What have you done with it? You are responsible for going to God to water it, read His Word, as Jesus said, "Eat of me". Jesus is the Word the Bread of Life. We must come to the Father daily to eat and partake of His nature, His wisdom, His presence and allow Him to grow the talent he placed in us.

Man's love or Phileo love is primarily about what it can get or do at the expense of others. It is selfish and based in self-righteousness. It is what Adam did after God asked him a very simple question;

Genesis 3
9 And the Lord God called unto Adam, and said unto him, Where art thou? 10 And he said, I heard thy voice in the garden, and I was afraid, because I was naked; and I hid myself. 11 And he said, Who told thee that thou wast naked? Hast thou eaten of the tree, whereof I commanded thee that thou shouldest not eat? 12 And the man said, The woman whom thou gavest to be with me, she gave me of the tree, and I did eat.

Adam shifted blame to someone else, Adam was protecting his own rear. He blamed the nearest person he could. This was a result of the fallen man already. Phileo love is self-serving, self-defensive, selfish love. Phileo love is avaricious and greedy. It seeks its own and wants for itself.

Thank you Jesus! We do not have to live that way anymore. We have grown up in it and lived in a secular fallen world, we may have to unlearn a lot, but we do not have to stay there!

Ephesians 5
Be ye therefore followers of God, as dear children; 2 And walk in love,

1 Cor 14
Follow after charity, and desire spiritual gifts,

The word love used in Ephesians is Agape and in Corinthians it is Agape. It is not just a character trait. It is who we are to follow, and in doing so who we become like as we follow. We are to learn how to walk in Agape, the nature and essence of God himself.

John said God is Love (1 John 4:8) and God is spirit

We who are born again are not just supposed to have the character traits of Love, the God kind of love, we are supposed to become like Him. We are supposed to be transformed into the same nature of our Father --

To be what He is. He is Love. He is Agape. We are to practice Love on a daily basis and as we do the nature of Love, the nature of God Himself, will become part of who we are. We will then become what Paul said in Romans 8, If we are to be spiritual beings, spiritual sons of God then we should begin at some point to take on the nature and presence of God. The nature of God. John said God is Agape, not just a character trait but a being. He is not loving simply because He likes love, God is Love because it is who He is. We enter into the practice of becoming love by faith on a daily basis as we encounter others and demonstrate that love nature we have learned in private with Him.

Romans 8:19
19 For the earnest expectation of the creature waiteth for the manifestation of the sons of God.

The sons of God are not just character trait people, they are like their Father. They abide in Him and in doing so become like Him. All of creation is waiting for this revealing of the sons and daughters of God to be revealed. They will be born again creatures of Love. Not just nice people who treat others well, but spiritual beings who worship Him in Spirit and truth, in Love. They have followed after, practiced love and in doing so have sunk their roots deep, wide, high and long into the nature of God - Love.

Psalm 1
Blessed is the man that walketh not in the counsel of the ungodly, nor standeth in the way of sinners, nor sitteth in the seat of the scornful. 2 But his delight is in the law of the Lord; and in his law doth he meditate day and night. 3 And he shall be like a tree planted by the rivers of water, that bringeth forth his fruit in his season; his leaf also shall not wither; and whatsoever he doeth shall prosper.

I don't know about you but that sounds like a great thing. To meditate on the law of God! That as a New Covenant born again child of God is the law of Love! Meditate on it day and night and look what will happen to you.

Eph 3
16 That he would grant you, according to the riches of his glory, to be strengthened with might by his Spirit in the inner man; 17 That Christ may dwell in your hearts by faith; that ye, being rooted and grounded in love, 18 May be able to comprehend with all saints what is the breadth, and length, and depth, and height; 19 And to know the love of Christ, which passeth knowledge, that ye might be filled with all the fulness of God.

By being rooted and grounded in Love, you are abiding in Him. You will grow in your inner man, the real you, the one that was born again and is Spirit. The everlasting part of you that is born again needs to grow into the image it was created for. As you mediate on His Love day and night and practice the law of Love (Agapao) you will become full of Him, as Paul said "the fullness of God" The Fullness of God is Agape! I find it interesting that Jesus also said, "if you abide in me and my words or command abide in you, my father and I will make our abode in you". If you follow this command to walk in love, you will be filled to the fullest extent of God possible; but you must abide in Him.

You cannot abide in Him if you do not obey His command. That's why David was accepted but Saul was not. It is about love! Love will make you desire to please Him and in doing so obey Him!

1John 2
3 And hereby we do know that we know him, if we keep his commandments. 4 He that saith, I know him, and keepeth not his commandments, is a liar, and the truth is not in him. 5 But whoso keepeth his word, in him verily is the love of God perfected: hereby know we that we are in him. 6 He that saith he abideth in him ought himself also so to walk, even as he walked. 7 Brethren, I write no new commandment unto you, but an old commandment which ye had from the beginning (Arche). The old commandment is the word which ye have heard from the beginning.

The command is the command of Love

John 13:34
34 A new commandment I give unto you, That ye love one another;

as I have loved you, that ye also love one another. 35 By this shall all men know that ye are my disciples, if ye have love one to another.

The world will know we are His disciples not by our character traits we sometimes walk in, but by the nature and presence of Love in us. God is love and if we obey His commands then we are told He will make His home in us. If He lives in us, wouldn't He take care of everything? Would we not bear in, on and through us the presence of God? The nature of God.

I find iT amazing that the Scriptures here that we used, tell us something else. That the commandment was old, it is from the beginning. This means love was around from the commencement of all things. How is that? Because God is Love, the first and the last, with no beginning and no end, love always was and always will be. Agape has always been. Agape created man in His image, in His likeness. That man gave it away and a second man was born who took it back and opened the door for us to walk, live, and eventually have our being in it. The law or existence of Love was long before Abraham, Moses and the law. It is the law that was written on our hearts when we became born again. It is the blueprint of how we should rebuild ourselves out of a fallen world and into a new Spiritual life. A born again life.

The law of love was and always will exist. It cannot be done away with or written out of existence. It is what we are to become through Christ. We are to become like we once were prior to the Fall, created in His image and through Christ we shall find our way back to His image: The image of Agape, the nature and being of God.

We are to love

John 3"7

Beloved, let us love one another: for love is of God; and every one that loveth is born of God, and knoweth God. 8 He that loveth not knoweth not God; for God is love.

Character is a symptom of the nature the controls you...

Guard Your Heart

Not everyone you meet is supposed to hang around you. Not everyone has good hearted desires. Most people are right down the middle for the most part. They're unaware that they even are missing something. Most people are not aware that no matter what you do in life, you are making disciples of some sort. People are always watching. The government systems of the earth are making disciples. We don't call them that, but when a person become dependent upon government for long term needs to be met, the government has rules and a way of doing things. Some governments want people dependent on purpose to get votes, change society or some other agenda. God wants us to choose to be dependent on Him for all we are and all we do.

In walking with God we are to be solely dependent on Him. There are unfortunately within the body, people who are not what they express themselves to be. They have an agenda. They want control, they want money, they want people to follow them. Whatever their motivation, we are not required to associate with them. I will always be polite but will not open my home and heart to them.

Proverbs 4
20 My son, attend to my words; incline thine ear unto my sayings. 21 Let them not depart from thine eyes; keep them in the midst of thine heart. 22 For they are life unto those that find them, and health to all their flesh. 23 Keep thy heart with all diligence; for out of it are the issues of life. 24 Put away from thee a froward mouth, and perverse lips put far from thee.

Just because you walk in love it does not make you a door mat. Do not allow people into your life and heart just because they seem great, wise, or even a Christian. Guard your heart for out of it flow the issues of life. Do not let others deposit in you junk that can hurt you. Stay away from gossipers, storytellers, people who seem to stir up strife. Just don't have anything to do with them. You cannot stop them from saying and doing things against you but that is not your concern. You cannot stop others from thinking thoughts. Don't participate in that system that lets us be controlled by thoughts and attitudes towards others. That is in opposition to how God see others.

I used to get so upset when someone lied about me. It has happened to all of us. I wanted to correct it and defend myself and let everyone know that the other person was a fraud. I'm not concerned about them anymore. Matter of fact I have found that by ignoring the dumb stuff, that person has really empowered me. I now pray over them, speak blessing over them, pray for a laborer to cross their path who can reach them. I cry out to God for them and not against them anymore. I have cried out to God about what others had done, said and say about me. Not anymore. I will love them into the right way. Sometimes we are not the person that is going to reach them, sometimes we have to stay away. For many of us that means we allow someone else to reach our relatives.

Recently I ran into a man twice who I chose not to speak to or even approach as he had caused my family and me much harm. I have heard others say, "I felt so bad not speaking to so and so but I just did not want the argument." It could be worded a number of ways. I chose not to speak to that man because I know better than to stick my hand in a wolf's mouth. I have peace about not entertaining him and allowing him to drop some rumor or lie in my head. It is my job to guard my heart, my kid's hearts, and my wife's heart. Love always protects. But someone might say, but you ignored that man, you did not act in love. Really? So you think I am supposed to act as if he is a brother even though he continues to walk in a doctrine that allows him to try to destroy others? He has proven himself to be destructive, divisive and a gossip. His actions are his testimony, not his words. No I do not need to entertain that or open myself and my family up to more attacks. Read what 2 John says

2 John
9 Whosoever transgresseth, and abideth not in the doctrine of Christ, hath not God. He that abideth in the doctrine of Christ, he hath both the Father and the Son. 10 If there come any unto you, and bring not this doctrine, receive him not into your house, neither bid him God speed: 11 For he that biddeth him God speed is partaker of his evil deeds.

The doctrine of Christ is Love.

In John 14 Jesus Himself tells us to abide in Him and His word and God will make His home in us. That is abiding in Love. Here John tells us in verse 10, if someone brings you something other than the doctrine of Love, do not let him into your house and don't even wish him God speed. Listen my friend, inordinate affection is all about words, and it is not the action and nature of love. It places feelings over the truth. You cannot separate Love and Truth. You cannot let everyone into your life, especially those whom have not the doctrine of Love. It is ok to stay away from trouble makers and those who do not follow after love. Love will not let you invite a wolf into your house. If you do you can expect to clean up a mess afterwards. Love protects, as husbands and parents we must protect our families, guard our hearts and only feed on the Word of God. If I see that man in an accident, I would be the first to stop, I'd stop for anyone, but I will not invite him into my life, home or family to spread the disease of false love.

Hope that helps, don't be condemned for walking in Love, protecting, edifying and lifting others up, stay away from those who tear down, gossip, preach some doctrine that is apart from the nature of God. Love. Be careful to not repeat a matter about others and spread any kind of unwholesome talk about another person. They are the children of God still and have the mercy of God to choose up until their last breath.

When meeting people we do not just jump on them and try to determine their entire character and nature in one meeting. We allow relationships to form and in that process we sometimes get burned and used and despitefully used. There are people who will take advantage of you simply because they know you will "walk in Love". They have a misconstrued opinion of Love. Listen, love protects and guards those it loves. It does not make you a door mat. Love is tough but not rough.

Love will protect. In the last days there are many people within the church worried about the antichrist and the growing darkness. Stop that! Part of how darkness works is in that others will despitefully use you, backbite and abuse you. You have the power to choose to be offended and hurt. We are told to walk through the valley of the shadow of death, not stop and study it, not repeat the matter to everyone else. Walk through, walk in love. He will protect you, He will encamp around you. Did not God put a hedge of protection around Job?

Job 1

Then Satan answered the Lord, and said, Doth Job fear God for nought? 10 Hast not thou made an hedge about him, and about his house, and about all that he hath on every side? thou hast blessed the work of his hands, and his substance is increased in the land.

God's testimony as well as that of the devil was that God protected Job. God put His hedge of protection around Job. Why? Well God's Himself gives testimony that Job in verse 8
And the Lord said unto Satan, Hast thou considered my servant Job, that there is none like him in the earth, a perfect and an upright man, one that feareth God, and escheweth evil?

Listen Job was not a Levite, a preacher, a man with specialized knowledge that no one else had. He was a man who simple walked in the law of love. Remember no one ever was perfect where the law was concerned. So how did Job do it? He understood walking in Love. He was in right standing with God because he ran from the world and evil. He was upright and perfect because he walked in Love with God. Go through the Word and look up the words, shield, hedge, protection and you will see that really all it is, is the presence of God Himself. If we make God our pursuit and follow after love, if we make obeying the original command the desire of our heart He will make His home in us. He will be our shield our buckler our protection. And the devil would give the same witness about us that he did about Job. God wants to protect, provide, to prosper us even in the end times no matter how dark the world gets. Arise and shine and let the Glory of God come upon you. See how gross darkenss covers the earth, well don't fret, time to arise and shine!

It is not very hard to see the results of the Love walk. Give it a try, follow after it ..

Galatians 5
6 For in Jesus Christ neither circumcision availeth anything, nor uncircumcision; but faith which worketh by love.

Some versions say, "the only thig that matters is faith expressing itself through love" That word is Agape. Through our potential nature that resides in us. Without the nature of love in us we cannot walk in Love.

Love will cause you to want to walk in the "things of God"and eskew or hate evil. Remember what God said of Job. Even the devil repeated it. That word eskew in the original Hebrew also has a definition that is "to rebel against." Job rebelled against evil! Love will cause you to run from things that are not God and to things that are of God. Yes there is a whole world out there that needs to hear the Gospel, but there are also a lot of folks in our own backyard who have heard the Gospel and chosen to walk in opposition to it. The Bible is very clear about the goats, the foolish shepards, and such. You will know them by their love walk. If they hold to a doctrine or some teaching over walking in Love they are off. Plain and simple. God's call is for each of us to be rooted and grounded in love.

One thing that I need to mention and I hope it fits here. God created one race, the human race, not a bunch of different human races. One race. We have to see other people as He sees them. Look past the actions and the skin colors. Turn off the media that promotes that junk. All of us are His children and He wants none to perish. That is His heart. When we look down on others, treat others as if we are better than them, we actually are pitting ourselves against the desire of God. I am a young man in many ways but I have studied enough church history as well as the Bible and one thing I am convinced of. God does not like it when we mistreat one of His children, saved or unsaved. We are all His children and He will defend them. It may not happen when you do it but God will remove an abusive man or women who is hurting His children. You may be able to call yourself anointed, but remember, He is their Father as well as yours. He will defend them from the fleecing and the abuse of those both those who are worldly and those who hide in the church. If you are a child who has been hurt, move on, leave it in the past. Repent, get right with God and do whatever you have to do to protect your heart, your family and begin to grow. Do not let someone else's conduct keep you from growing relationship with Jesus. You are accountable to Him

    Let me make another comment that may upset some readers: I have had to correct this in my own life as well and am thankful for it. Removing the influence of the media from your life will help immensely. We know from the Word that we are supposed to find comfort in Him. In His Word, not the world. If you are spending all your spare time in front of the media,,.. you are being fed by the mindset of the fallen world. You are not guarding your heart. I am not saying that you cannot watch movies, Facebook etc... I am saying that if your thoughts and emotions are controlled by the world's opinion of things you are in danger. You must learn to depend on the Word not the world. The world will not tell you the truth. It will lead you down the path of darkness, there is no light in them. You will only find light in one place.
    Be at peace and protect your heart. I grew up hearing "if the people are all heading one way, look for another". Going against the grain is sometimes the wrong, but most of the time it is the right thing to do when the things of God are in play. The masses have proven it out over history that they keep getting it wrong. What is so special about this generation that makes us all think we are doing it right? I prefer to stay on bended knee and listen to what He says. Jesus did that and so should we. Protect your heart and protect your relationship with Him, your wife and your family. Always remember, how you treat others matters! One of my hero's is Cornelius out of the book of Acts. Study his life: How he treated others made a difference! It will for you too. God moved supernaturally for Him and all Gentiles will forever be grateful! He did not have right theology as he was not even born again, but he did walk in love and that was proven by what the angel said. Your giving and alms to the poor. Cornelius lived a life of giving and with no strings attached. Love is demonstrated in its forgiveness and giving. You do not have to have all perfect doctrine to be found and used by God! giving is about Love and the result is the return. We give because we love.
    There is a way that seems right unto man... be wary of it!

His Banner Over Me Is Love

Song of Solomon 2
4 He brought me to the banqueting house, and his banner over me was love.

This has always been one of my favorite Scriptures. His flag that He flies over me is love. He marks me as His with His flag. God's banner is a flag of Love; not only the action of love but the nature of love. That word love is the Hebrew word AHABAH. It is often used as a noun and refers to the nature and presence of God. It is His essence through and through, it is who He is from everlasting to everlasting. This is really the equivalent of the Greek word in the New Testament, Agape. The nature and presence of God Himself.

God set His flag over you. I went a little further one day and studied out the rest of the words in that sentence. The word banner is awesome! It is only used once in the entire Bible. I like words like that! It comes from the Hebrew root word DAGAL (daw-gal) which means a flag, but not just a marker flag but a conspicuous flag everyone can see God"s banner! The word banner used here in Song of Solomon is the word DEGEL (deh-gel) Used only once it speaks of a standard. So we could say that that verse could also read, He places a conspicuous standard over me that all can see!

Want an example of that? Job

Job 1
1 There was a man in the land of Uz, whose name was Job; and that

man was perfect and upright, and one that feared God, and eschewed evil. 2 And there were born unto him seven sons and three daughters. 3 His substance also was seven thousand sheep, and three thousand camels, and five hundred yoke of oxen, and five hundred she asses, and a very great household; so that this man was the greatest of all the men of the east. 4 And his sons went and feasted in their houses, every one his day; and sent and called for their three sisters to eat and to drink with them. 5 And it was so, when the days of their feasting were gone about, that Job sent and sanctified them, and rose up early in the morning, and offered burnt offerings according to the number of them all: for Job said, It may be that my sons have sinned, and cursed God in their hearts. Thus did Job continually. 6 Now there was a day when the sons of God came to present themselves before the Lord, and Satan came also among them. 7 And the Lord said unto Satan, Whence comest thou? Then Satan answered the Lord, and said, From going to and fro in the earth, and from walking up and down in it. 8 And the Lord said unto Satan, Hast thou considered my servant Job, that there is none like him in the earth, a perfect and an upright man, one that feareth God, and escheweth evil? 9 Then Satan answered the Lord, and said, Doth Job fear God for nought? 10 Hast not thou made an hedge about him, and about his house, and about all that he hath on every side? thou hast blessed the work of his hands, and his substance is increased in the land.

So the story begins with the fact that Job was a man who feared God walked upright before God and ran from Evil. He did not allow evil , he did not cover evil, he ran from it. If you study out that word eskew in the Hebrew, one meaning is to rebel. Job rebelled against Evil! How nice would that be to hear that preached instead of how much humans rebel against God! God Himself says that Job was upright. You cannot be upright without loving God. The love relationship is what gets us to that place. When we love someone we will trust them, honor them, respect them, follow them, communicate with them, have intimacy with them and on and on and on.

Job was a man who loved God with all his heart, soul and strength and what does the devil say? Even the devil has to admit that Job had something -- a hedge of protection. Job was protected. He was blessed. He was being run down and overtaken by the blessing of God. Job knew it/ The devil knew it and God gave testimony of it. God had placed His banner over Job. God revealed Himself in and through the life of Job. He wants to do the same for you and me.

Job obviously had to have understood the everlasting law. Love. He wanted nothing to do with evil, he wanted to please the one whom he loved and who showered His love on him.

The banner God wants to place over us is not just some small marker that we see used to mark underground lines and such. It is a large standard that the whole world can see and will notice. We are not to hide what God has done to us, it is conspicuous and on display for all to see. We are so blessed and outrageously overrun by the blessings of God that the whole world and even the devil himself notices. God's banner is that standard. Love is the nature and presence of God. The word love used in this statement -- His banner over me is love -- is the nature of God, not just the law of love.

Psalm 3
3 But thou, O Lord, art a shield for me; my glory, and the lifter up of mine head.

Psalm 5
12 For thou, Lord, wilt bless the righteous; with favour wilt thou compass him as with a shield.

Psalm 7
My defence is of God, which saveth the upright in heart.

There are so many Scriptures that refer to God wanting to care for us, to protect us, to defend us, to love us! Will we let Him? He wants to show us off! He wants to demonstrate to the World that there is a God in Heaven. He is looking for men and women through whom He can do this!

Obeying His command of love causes the nature of love to take up residence in us. In Job's day it was over him and around him, in our New Testament experience it is in us and around us and all over us. When we do as Jesus said, obey my commands, then my Father and I will make our abode, (home) in you. When God moves in, He brings all His blessings with Him. Those blessing are so conspicuous that the whole world will take notice.

God is not wanting to just put a flag over you, like an army battalion or company on the march, no army hides their flag or colors. They put them out front as they advance. God wants to place His banner, His standard out front and over us that the entire world has no problem distinguishing whose we are.

Recall what is says in Deuteronomy 28

Deuteronomy 28
1 And it shall come to pass, if thou shalt hearken diligently unto the voice of the Lord thy God, to observe and to do all his commandments which I command thee this day, that the Lord thy God will set thee on high above all nations of the earth:2 And all these blessings shall come on thee, and overtake thee, if thou shalt hearken unto the voice of the Lord thy God.

I love that chapter of the Bible. Here God is telling them that if they obey the law or the commandments, He will cause His blessing to run us down and over take us. For the New Testament believer the law is the Law of Love. The law that always was and always will be. He says something else in that chapter that is so key. Twice in the above Scripture he used the word harken. Or listen to the voice of the Spirit. For us the New Covenant believer that is listening to the voice of the Spirit. Or we could say, being led by His Spirit. He will guide us and teach us and protect us, if we will obey His law. That is it. Obey the Law of Love, the law that has always been and He will cause all the blessing of Deuteronomy 28 to run you down and over take you!

I have a friend who is beginning to experience this. He does not dress to the nines. He is not the most proficient reader or speaker. He dresses like an old farmer. He drives old repaired cars, yet he is honest, forthright, loves God and loves people. He will help anyone. Here in this country we often see people in need of a "lift", he always gives lifts. He helps others and will often recruit others to go help people in need. He gives and gives and loves to love. I know personally he has many a nights he does not get a lot of sleep as he is up talking with God. I asked some friends the other day "What's happening with him?" One said he was being elevated. Someone else said, "It's the anointing." In Biblical terms, he is being run down and overtaken. He has had so many things happen to him that he is awestruck and so are people around him. He has contracts come to him. He has land offered to him. He has many more examples of how the blessing is running him down. God honors the man who honors Him and His Word. This friend may not be seen at first appearance as much, but God sees him differently. He does everything he can to stay in love. He will not white lie, as some say that is good business. He will not manipulate or represent himself for more than he is. Yes he's been taken advantage of, but he let that go. He walks in love, even when no one else understands or agrees with him. He sought God's way and not man's way. Now men are taking notice.

Did God not do the same with David and with the might men of valor? With Jesus? How about you? Move your free will out of the way and allow Him to place His banner over you. Allow Him to become the strong tower, the shadow over you. Allow Him to lead you and guide you, follow His command and it will happen.

His Disciples A Display Of His Splendor

John 13

31 Therefore, when he was gone out, Jesus said, Now is the Son of man glorified, and God is glorified in him. 32 If God be glorified in him, God shall also glorify him in himself, and shall straightway glorify him. 33 Little children, yet a little while I am with you. Ye shall seek me: and as I said unto the Jews, Whither I go, ye cannot come; so now I say to you. 34 A new commandment I give unto you, That ye love one another; as I have loved you, that ye also love one another. 35 By this shall all men know that ye are my disciples, if ye have love one to another.

I love this Scripture, it has brought me so much insight and revelation. Jesus is spending His last few minutes with the disciples and He tells them the secret to everything: A new command. Now we need to examine that word new, because it really doesn't mean new in the original Greek as we read in the English. It is the Greek word Kainos, which actually means to renew, Similar to going back to the library to renew the check out on a book you have already had. This word also has a root to it that brings with it a meaning to renew something that already was. Jesus did not introduce a brand new commandment here. He was renewing the original commandment. That commandment is the one that was in the beginning. Love is and has always existed. It will always be here. It cannot be done away with or cease to exist. It never was non-existent. Unfortunately, the people of Israel forgot the ancient ways and had to be reminded.

Jesus renewed the original command and fulfilled the Levitical law for us. The original command is the greatest because it always was and will forever be. It is what Adam had and now we have.

Jerimiah 31
3 The Lord hath appeared of old unto me, saying, Yea, I have loved thee with an everlasting love: therefore with lovingkindness have I drawn thee.

God is everlasting to everlasting and since God is Love, so is love. Here the word Jerimiah used as the same Hebrew word that refers to the nature of love. Often used as a noun. God is love and always will be.

Going back to the John 13:34, Jesus used the word Agapao meaning the command is to act, practice, demonstrate, and pursue love towards God and others. He said that by this all men will know you are my disciples. I love that word disciples. You see in the old days, a scribe, lawyer or student of the law were identified by the doctrine they had. For instance, there were Pharisee, Sadducee, Maccabees, etc, each sect or denomination held to a little different beliefs about the law and the coming Messiah. Much like today, if you meet someone who is Christian you can identify what domination they subscribe to by the teaching and doctrines they hold dear. Each domination has differences and often they separate us. But here Jesus is saying, "Hey guys, there is one thing that will let everyone know you are my students, my followers, my children. Love. Because you love others, you love God the whole world will know you are my students. Isn't that amazing? I wonder if is still applicable today? Of course it is the law of love always was and always will be applicable. It was what was in the beginning and cannot be undone. The proof of your discipleship is not a degree, it is fruit of love that brings glory to God!

But let's go deeper into what Jesus said. First in verse 34, He refers to the command. He used the Word Agapao. Meaning the command is to demonstrate, practice love to one another. We could read that verse like this.

I renew an old command with you, That you practice and demonstrate the God kind of love toward one another; as I have demonstrated my love towards you, that ye also continue to demonstrate, practice and walk in love towards one another.

The command is to Agapao: To demonstrate towards God and all men, with all our heart, soul and strength the passion of love.

Now on to verse 35. Here Jesus changes the word love to agape, meaning the nature and fullness of God Himself. God is love. God is Agape. This is the noun. We could read verse 35 this way

By this shall all men know that ye are my students and followers, if ye have produced the nature and presence of God in you and towards others?

We begin with practicing the precepts of the original, ancient, renewed old commandment and we become like our Father, the image we were originally created to be. It will require all your heart, soul and strength to walk in Love. Your mind will not understand it all, your flesh will want to defend itself. You will be abused and hurt by those close to you. The attacks will come from the enemy and he will use those close to you to do it. Stay in love, know that the attacks are from the enemy.

When people attack, you can fight for your right to defend yourself or you can ask God what He would do. God's will is that all would come to repentance and maturity. Sometimes defending your right to be right will actually cause more harm. There are times you have to walk away, turn it over to God and let Him handle it. Recently we had to make another decision along those lines, the other persons involved can think whatever they want, but because we walked in love and in agreement with what God wanted, it was almost as we had walked right up to the devil's face, took the gun out of his hand and disarmed him. We gained the victory by walking in love. Yes there are times to stand your ground, but remember that God's love outweighs our opinion of others. Winning a battle in the court of justice or opinion will not bring restoration, doing it God's way will. You cannot stop people from thinking or saying whatever they want, your testimony is based on actions and deeds not words.

You see that you will be known by others by the fruit you produce, Love. That is the fruit of the born again child of God. Here is the neat thing, you will produce fruit, in season, and there are some places prophetically in the Word that tell us that we will produce in every season during the last days! You will be known by others by your fruit. Your identity is not the fruit. Who you are will be who you are no matter what others see. Your identity is not in the fruit, it is in your nature. Jesus said that if we make the tree good, we will produce good fruit. We are not supposed to focus on the fruit, but on the nature of the tree. Too many people are attacking, dodging or trying to change the fruit of people instead of changing the nature that causes the bad fruit. You are love, because your nature was changed, born again into the love nature that mankind once had. The image that was deposited in you is the nature and image of God, Love. That nature is there, we have to exercise it and develop it, feed it and nourish it. A tree will not grow if we do not feed it and water it. That being the Spirit and the Word. Then the Gardener will prune it and make it more fruitful. We allow Him and others to see the fruit and use it for the sake of others, not ourselves. We focus on the tree. Care for the man on the inside of you, the real man, the spirit man and you will become a love fruit bearing tree. Focus on making the tree healthy and it will produce healthy fruit after its own kind. You are a love tree and by staying in vital living contact with the vine you will grow and become what all of creation is waiting for.

John 15
1 I am the true vine, and my Father is the husbandman. 2 Every branch in me that beareth not fruit he taketh away: and every branch that beareth fruit, he purgeth it, that it may bring forth more fruit. 3 Now ye are clean through the word which I have spoken unto you. 4 Abide in me, and I in you. As the branch cannot bear fruit of itself, except it abide in the vine; no more can ye, except ye abide in me. 5 I am the vine, ye are the branches: He that abideth in me, and I in him, the same bringeth forth much fruit: for without me ye can do nothing. 6 If a man abide not in me, he is cast forth as a branch, and is withered; and men gather them, and cast them into the fire, and they are burned. 7 If ye abide in me, and my words abide in you, ye shall ask what ye will, and it shall be done unto you. 8 Herein is my Father glorified, that ye bear much fruit; so shall ye be my disciples.

An apple tree is not identified only when it has apples on it. The display of its identity is the splendor of apples! An apple trees nature is what produced the apples. Apple trees can be identified in and out of season. The harvest of fruit is a symptom of being an apple tree. The old man which was under the law of sin had a sin nature, we were all born with it and raised in it. We had to be born again. We had to be given a new nature, not just new fruit. We had to be re born, into the original nature of man who was made in the image of God, who is a Spirit and Who is Love. We were born out of the sin dominated world and into the Love kingdom. We are creatures of love, because we received that nature of Love. Now you may have controversy with yourself and God and even be unbearable to others, because you refuse to live according to the new nature. Maybe you have never heard who you truly are now. Maybe you have been born again and yet all you hear is a sin nature message. Begin to develop that real you, the one on the inside that will live forever and you will begin to grow into the image and nature of your Fathe. In time you will produce fruit keeping in line with that true nature. You will see others differently, you will see yourself differently, you will walk in the ways of God who is love and not according to the way that seems right to men. The way of love is the greatest possible journey we can make! Your mind will give you fits. That is ok, that is the spiritual battle, run to the Word, run into dependency on Him. Stay with it and you will find that you are living the narrow path that does not need to look for loopholes in this Christianity thing, but will enjoy the journey and the relationship it develops in you. If you're married, well...that gets so much more fun, better, too the best!!! Love leads you into that life that is worth living!

It can be turned on and turned away from because we each have free will but Love will always be there. It is the ancient path.

Jerimiah 6:16

16 Thus saith the Lord, Stand ye in the ways, and see, and ask for the ancient paths, where is the good way, and walk therein, and ye shall find rest for your souls. But they said, We will not walk therein.

Song of Songs

8: 5 Who is this that cometh up from the wilderness, leaning upon her beloved? I raised thee up under the apple tree: there thy mother brought thee forth: there she brought thee forth that bare thee. 6 Set me as a seal upon thine heart, as a seal upon thine arm: for love is strong as death; jealousy is cruel as the grave: the coals thereof are coals of fire, which hath a most vehement flame. 7 Many waters cannot quench love, neither can the floods drown it: if a man would give all the substance of his house for love, it would utterly be contemned.

It is time for the church to come out of the wilderness and learn to lean upon the Lord Jesus. Time for total dependency on God. Love is the key to the kingdom. Finding our way with Him will answer the questions of the heart. Solomon goes on to compare love to death. Many have heard the expression that "everyone must pay taxes and die" In reality everyone must learn to Love, sooner or later and then pass on. If you don't learn the way of Love in this earth, what do you think you will be doing when you get to the sweet by and by. Just because you have fire insurance, you're spared from hell, does not make you a mature son or daughter. . In spiritual reality, you have to Ahabah. You have to take on the nature and presence of Love! Only love has such a demand and desire on the human being. Only Agape and Ahabah will satisfy that emptiness and longing that you wake up with. There is too much in the Scriptures about our responsibility as children of God. Do not just settle for the easy path the "I'm good to go path" Some will make it by the skin of their chinny chin chin, others will walk in and hear the desired words. Some will, as I heard on preacher say, "Well... Done" Other will hear "Well done my good and faithful servant".

The Hebrew word for love in verse six and seven is the word Ahabah. That is the nature and essence of who God is. Often used in the same manner that Agape is used in the Greek. As we grow in Christ, in Love the passions and the desires of love overcome us. We become a lover of God and men. We care about things we never cared about. We see things differently, we hunger for more of him and his ways. We do not want to be out of His presence. We want all of Him we can get. You will find that even your desires of things you thought you wanted will change. He truly knows the desires of your heart! That is the secret of Song of Songs. It is a picture of the spiritual journey from brand new baby in Christ to full grown bride of Christ. In the beginning our vineyards have little to no fruit they are unkempt and full of weeds, as we grow we see more fruit and less weeds, we are asked to do things with Him, like the Shulamite women we might at first refuse but then we repent and go out looking for him, We find him and obey Him and we fall more madly in love. It is not reasonable, it is not on man's wisdom, it is spiritual. It is love. Throughout the song you see that she is dancing with him and He supports her, he cares for her, then as you approach the end of the song He doesn't just call her His love, He calls her His bride. There is a growing process, we must yield to. Then one day as we have matured we cross out of the wilderness, leaning on our beloved, depending on him, we learn to be led by His Spirit and love.

Notice that love is stronger than death, it has to be otherwise we are all lost. Love conquers and cannot be defeated. It may not battle that way man has been taught but it cannot be defeated. Love is such a strong fire that even another flood can not quench it! Love is so massively awesome that it cannot lose. If that kind of power were unleashed on the Earth! Yes Jesus demonstrated it in His life, death and resurrection! He then gave it to us. He gave us a portion of it to each of us when we were born again and He like all of creation is waiting for us to discover it. Even the devil is expecting it, why else is he fighting so hard to keep us from fulfilling our destiny? He knows love defeated him once, and love has won, now it is all about keeping us blind to the truth with in us.

I cannot tell you that you will have the exact experience I had. You will not. I can tell you some of it, as you will have to come to an end of your ways, you will have to recognize the flesh cannot get you where you want to be. You will even develop a little distrust of a lot of what you've be led to believe up to now. He will not leave you nor forsake you, He is longing for you to enter into those deep waters and grow in dependency upon Him.

We must desire with all our heart and passion this Love, this being of Love. As you grow in hunger for it, it will be like a violent coal that cannot be put out. Another flood will not quench it. Love is powerful and strong. It is stronger than death. It drives sin and disease as far as the east is from the west. As you come to know the length, breath depth and height of the love of God, which you will never find the end of, you will find that Love keeps pushing that old past history of sin further and further from you. You can be free and you can walk in it. Love cannot fail. If we chose to walk in it. It is all still about free will. Adam had it and so do you. Exercise it for the plans and purposes of God and He will meet you.

There is a place that you fall so dependent upon God that you do not want anything else. Isaiah stated in Isaiah 3

Isaiah 3
3 And shall make him of quick understanding in the fear of the Lord: and he shall not judge after the sight of his eyes, neither reprove after the hearing of his ears:

Jesus fulfilled this prophecy in John 5

19 Then answered Jesus and said unto them, Verily, verily, I say unto you, The Son can do nothing of himself, but what he seeth the Father do: for what things soever he doeth, these also doeth the Son likewise. 20 For the Father loveth the Son, and sheweth him all things that himself doeth: and he will shew him greater works than these that ye may marvel.

Jesus then told us in John 16

John 16
7 Nevertheless I tell you the truth; It is expedient for you that I go away: for if I go not away, the Comforter will not come unto you; but if I depart, I will send him unto you.

Then Verse 13

13 Howbeit when he, the Spirit of truth, is come, he will guide you into all truth: for he shall not speak of himself; but whatsoever he shall hear, that shall he speak: and he will shew you things to come. 14 He shall glorify me: for he shall receive of mine, and shall shew it unto you. 15 All things that the Father hath are mine: therefore said I, that he shall take of mine, and shall shew it unto you.

Jesus was the fulfillment of the prophecy of Isaiah and then Jesus told us that we could and would do the same thing as He. We can do nothing in and of ourselves. We must be dependent upon the Holy Spirit just as Jesus was. We must learn to lean upon our Lord in all we do and all we say. We must lean upon Him. Not the world's way not the knowledge of Good but the Truth. We must live that life that personal one on one relationship that bring about revelation and not just knowledge.

You see truth without Agape is actually knowledge. Truth with Agape brings revelation. Revelation is based on the relationship that birthed it. Knowledge puffs up, love builds up. God builds others up, he will build you up and let you lean on Him and walk with Him. He already knows you, He wants you to know Him and pursue Him, then your life will be the best life now, not just for you but for others. God wants to show you in His love (1John 3:1) He is that kind of God. He is wooing you and wants to enter into a romance with each of us. He loves us that much. We have to be willing to follow His rules and His program. I should say, we need to follow His rules of courtship, not ours. We have to seek Him and want Him. He is a gentleman and will not force you to do anything. You can sense the tug down deep and you know it. Hand yourself over to Him so He can show you the wonders of His ways!

If you want it and you go for it..,, God will meet you and fill you. Jesus said everything depends or hangs on this principle of life. Love. Jesus made it the cornerstone of His ministry and everything He did. He loved, and He said, "If you love me you will obey me" To obey Jesus is to be totally dependent on Him for all you are and all you do. Can you do that? Can you yield to Him? It is the path that is the purest and the most adventuresome. It is the greatest journey we will ever take. To love others and God. You may not be able to handle it. You may not be able to give up the World way of doing things. You may not want to exercise the discipline to follow after Love, but it will lead you into the freedom you desire. Whatever you decide please stick to it, don't be luke warm or mushy. The Church does not need more secular Christians. Get on fire, make the choice and begin the walk in Love. Run if you must. And as you go remember one thing... It is His harvest not ours!

Jesus said in Matthew 5

Mattheew 5
6 Blessed are they which do hunger and thirst after righteousness: for they shall be filled.

Today take the love letter He wrote to you. Read some, read it out loud, go verse by verse and ask Him what He means. If you have to take love Scriptures that we quote in the next chapter and highlight them, color code them with a color pencil, read those over and over until it sinks down deep. Your prayer life may be cold and dull, but talk to God about each of these verses as if you where the one they were written to. Ask Him about them. Pray over them. Then go out in public and live like you believe them. Your romance may not change overnight but it will grow and you will know it! He loves you so much and He wants to be your beloved as you are His! He has time for you and is waiting! He loves to support us and care for us, He loves to dance with us. Let Him become your first love again! Give Him time to transform you and watch what happens! Get hungry for romance as you've never known it.

Hudson Taylor wrote, "The Holy Spirit never creates hungering's and thirsting's after righteousness, but in order that Christ may fill the longing soul."

1 John 4:
8 He that loveth not knoweth not God; for God is love.

He that Agapao not knowth not God, for God is Agape!

Love The Most Misunderstood Word In the Bible

As mentioned earlier there are many words in the Aramaic, Hebrew and Greek that we translate in to some version of one word... Love. Love is overlooked as simple, as weak, as not spiritually deep, lacking in the supernatural. In reality Love is the basis and the foundation of the Christ-like life. We enjoy enthusiastic worship services; but, the foundation is not emotional services, not rules, not lack of rules, not feel good atmosphere, but Love is solid, truthful, deep and wide and high. Love is protective and yet understanding. No. The foundation is Love. Love is not just a rule either. It is a Being. As Christ-like ones we are supposed to be transformed from selfish self-protecting beings (flesh), into the Christ like nature of Love (Spirit). Love is not just a golden rule, it is not just a good idea, it is true Spiritual maturity. Paul said, let us go on to perfection, in Love. He said let us follow after love, make it our life's journey, Jesus said all of the law and the prophets hinge, hang onto, are supported by this law of Love. In speaking to the religious leaders of his day he told them, you missed the spirit behind the law. God is a Spirit, He is also Love. The Spirit of God is Love. The born again experience is to be born spiritually into Love and it is expected that we should grow in this love until we reach maturity. We are to become like our Father, recreated in His Spiritual image to become like Him. God id Love. As it says, "Jesus was the first born among many brethren".

Let examine a couple of the words from the Bible that are translated into some version of the word Love, some words are also translated into Charity. I want to specifically show you the difference in the two words Agape and Agapeo. Both can easily be referred to as the "love of God" but I want to show you a difference in the words and how they are used in Scripture to teach us something incredible. First let me begin to show you some Scripture on Agapao

Matt 22:36-40
36 Master, which is the great commandment in the law? 37 Jesus said unto him, Thou shalt love the Lord thy God with all thy heart, and with all thy soul, and with all thy mind. 38 This is the first and great commandment. 39 And the second is like unto it, Thou shalt love thy neighbour as thyself. 40 On these two commandments hang all the law and the prophets.

He is referring to the commandment and uses Agapao in both cases of the word love. He is referring to the verb of love, that demonstration and action of love.

Mark 12:29-34
28 And one of the scribes came, and having heard them reasoning together, and perceiving that he had answered them well, asked him, Which is the first commandment of all? 29 And Jesus answered him, The first of all the commandments is, Hear, O Israel; The Lord our God is one Lord:30 And thou shalt love the Lord thy God with all thy heart, and with all thy soul, and with all thy mind, and with all thy strength: this is the first commandment. 31 And the second is like, namely this, Thou shalt love thy neighbour as thyself. There is none other commandment greater than these. 32 And the scribe said unto him, Well, Master, thou hast said the truth: for there is one God; and there is none other but he:33 And to love him with all the heart, and with all the understanding, and with all the soul, and with all the strength, and to love his neighbour as himself, is more than all whole burnt offerings and sacrifices. 34 And when Jesus saw that he answered discreetly, he said unto him, Thou art not far from the kingdom of God.

Here He again only used the word Agapao, the action of love! Yet He tells the scribe, "your close" to understanding the secret!

Luke 6

31 And as ye would that men should do to you, do ye also to them likewise. 32 For if ye love them which love you, what thank have ye? for sinners also love those that love them. 33 And if ye do good to them which do good to you, what thank have ye? for sinners also do even the same. 34 And if ye lend to them of whom ye hope to receive, what thank have ye? for sinners also lend to sinners, to receive as much again. 35 But love ye your enemies, and do good, and lend, hoping for nothing again; and your reward shall be great, and ye shall be the children of the Highest: for he is kind unto the unthankful and to the evil. 36 Be ye therefore merciful, as your Father also is merciful.

Again this is the Agapao, verb of love. It requires an action, but He is clearly showing us that it is an intention of the heart that makes it so different. He also refers to a no strings attached kind of love. Agapao is not looking for a reward or a return, just loving people, loving others.

Luke 10:27

26 He said unto him, What is written in the law? how readest thou? 27 And he answering said, Thou shalt love the Lord thy God with all thy heart, and with all thy soul, and with all thy strength, and with all thy mind; and thy neighbour as thyself. 28 And he said unto him, Thou hast answered right: this do, and thou shalt live.

Again, this is the verb of love. Line upon line, precept upon precept, we demonstrate our commitment to God and others in the way we act toward them. He gives the promise of life here as well! Are you tired of a standard hum drum life? Are you like Job saying I do not just want to live, meaning sleep, eat, work and repeat.. or do you want to live the God kind of life, as Job said, I want to live! I want to Zoe, the fullness of life! Not just get through it! There is more to life than just getting by.

John 3

16 For God so loved the world, that he gave his only begotten Son, that whosoever believeth in him should not perish, but have everlasting life. 17 For God sent not his Son into the world to condemn the world;

but that the world through him might be saved.

Agapao is used in this passage. It is the demonstration of God's love for us. Love is chiefly demonstrated in us as it was in God through forgiveness and giving. No string attached forgiveness and giving. Don't give to get. Give to love.

John 13:34
34 A new commandment I give unto you, That ye love one another; as I have loved you, that ye also love one another. 35 By this shall all men know that ye are my disciples, if ye have love one to another.

Here He uses the word Agapao in reference to the command, remember that word new is actually the Greek word Kainos, which refers to renewing something that always was. This is not a new command as the English bible translated it, it is the original and first command, the command that is from everlasting to everlasting. Jesus is actually saying "I renew with you an old already existing command" Verse 35 is Agape!

John 14:15
15 If ye love me, keep my commandments.
Agapao

James 2:8
8 If ye fulfil the royal law according to the scripture, Thou shalt love thy neighbour as thyself, ye do well:

The demonstration and action of the verb Agapao! Wasn't it James who said let us love in action and truth and not words? Did not Matthew say "Wisdom is proved right by her actions?"

1Peter 1
22 Seeing ye have purified your souls in obeying the truth through the Spirit unto unfeigned love of the brethren, see that ye love one another with a pure heart fervently:

Agapao is not a fake or human love. It will cause you to mean what you say and do what you mean. It is the beginning of the sanctification process that purifies us and helps us obey the Spirit! Begin to walk in love today to the best of your ability, God can work with your best effort.

1 Petr 4:
8 And above all things have fervent charity among yourselves: for charity shall cover the multitude of sins.

Agapao will cover a multitude of sin. You can make mistakes, but at least try, then once your making the effort, He will cover you and protect you and help you. We have to be willing to get started.

1John 2
10 He that loveth his brother abideth in the light, and there is none occasion of stumbling in him.

Walking in love will help you not be a stumbling block for others. You will love others and in doing so as you will grow in the practice and nature of love. You will consider others and God's before yourself. It does not mean others will not use you and persecute you, but your response (not reaction) is what Love will govern.

You will note that every reference of scripture that uses the Greek word Agapao is in reference to an action. The Greek word Agapao is a verb. It denotes action or something we should do. In John 3:16 God demonstrated His love (agapao) for us in sending Jesus. I like to say it this way, Agapao is the demonstration and the practice of Love towards God and others. It is this daily walk that Paul referred as the most excellent way. As in 1 Cort 14:1, Paul said, let us pursue, or follow after this great love. It is our life's journey. It is the path of the most excellent way. It is the path that Jesus demonstrated for us. It is the path that the Holy Spirit will guide us in as we love (agapao) Him and others with all our heart soul and strength. You could say, how we practice love towards others at all cost and with all passion. Our demonstration of love to others is not about how they can bless us in return, but in demonstration with pure intent and all sincerity as Paul said. We must be sincere and feigning nothing in our pursuit of God and His ways and how we treat others. Agapao love is the demonstration, the daily conduct towards God and others. As we practice it on a daily basis, one day at a time, it begins to transform us and we become the spiritual beings we were meant to be originally.

In the Old Testament the command given in Leviticus to "Love God with all your heart, all your mind and all your strength" is the same command given in the New Testament That word love in Hebrew is Ahab. It also is used as a verb, often to describe the act or demonstration of love. The rest of the law was given to give understanding to that law. That is why Jesus said "all of the law and the prophets hang on this one command"

Now let's examine Agape

Agape is used in the following Scriptures, and you will notice that some of them have both agape and agapao which will address later in the chapter.

John 5:
42 But I know you, that ye have not the love of God in you.

He is referring to the Spirit and the nature of love, this is Agape. God Himself. If you do not love it is because you do not know Him.

John 13:
34 A new commandment I give unto you, That ye love one another; as I have loved you, that ye also love one another. 35 By this shall all men know that ye are my disciples, if ye have love one to another.

Verse 34 is Agapao, the action and daily demonstration of walking in love towards God and others. Verse 35 is referring to the nature and presence that we will be transformed into as we practice, pursue the love walk.

John 15
8 Herein is my Father glorified, that ye bear much fruit; so shall ye be my disciples. 9 As the Father hath loved me, so have I loved you: continue ye in my love. 10 If ye keep my commandments, ye shall abide in my love; even as I have kept my Father's commandments, and abide in his love. 11 These things have I spoken unto you, that my joy might remain in you, and that your joy might be full. 12 This is my commandment, That ye

love one another, as I have loved you. 13 Greater love hath no man than this, that a man lay down his life for his friends. 14 Ye are my friends, if ye do whatsoever I command you.

Verse 8 He is telling us that we will bring God much Glory if we bear the fruit, the fruit of what? Love, not Agapao but Agape. We bring the Father Glory by becoming like Him. That is how the world will know we are His disciples, His children. How? Verse 10, if we keep His commandment, and abide in His Agape. Abide in His nature. Jesus kept that same command and in doing so He abided in the Fathers nature, Agape. Verse 12 is agapao the commandment, verse 13 goes back to Agape, that nature of God. We are His friends if we mimic Him, Copy Him, do as He did, by obeying God and walking in Love. (John 17:26)

2Cort 13:
11 Finally, brethren, farewell. Be perfect, be of good comfort, be of one mind, live in peace; and the God of love and peace shall be with you. 12 Greet one another with an holy kiss. 13 All the saints salute you. 14 The grace of the Lord Jesus Christ, and the love of God, and the communion of the Holy Ghost, be with you all.

The agape of God, the nature and the presence of God.

Gal 5:
13 For, brethren, ye have been called unto liberty; only use not liberty for an occasion to the flesh, but by love serve one another. 14 For all the law is fulfilled in one word, even in this; Thou shalt love thy neighbour as thyself. 15 But if ye bite and devour one another, take heed that ye be not consumed one of another. 16 This I say then, Walk in the Spirit, and ye shall not fulfil the lust of the flesh.

We walk in Love if we obey the command and Agapao our neighbor, even our enemy. We walk in the Spirit when we walk in love because the Spirit is the Spirit and nature of Love. The Holy Spirit's nature is the same nature as the Father, love. You cannot walk in the Spirit without walking in love, but you can "walk in the spirit" with miracles signs and wonders for a time without walking in Love. It will not last but it will happen. Walking in Love is the most perfect way to walk in the Spirit.

That is whole point behind 1 Corthinans chapter 12 through 14.

Gal5:22
22 But the fruit of the Spirit is love,

I just stopped that verse after the word love. The word used here is Agape. The fruit of the Spirit in that entire sentence is singular. The rest of the items that follow after love are attributes of Agape. The fruit of the Spirit is Love. Pure and simple. You bite into an apple and you taste the joy (juice) the skin (self-Control) and on and on. The apple is the fruit. The fruit we are supposed to produce in our lives that proves our relationship and fellowship with the Father is Love. If we do that the rest will follow, "love, joy, peace, longsuffering, gentleness, goodness, faith, 23 Meekness, temperance: against such there is no law." There are no other Scriptures that support that there is no law against anything but love.

If I were to invite you to my house for a party and asked you to bring a dish, you would not show up with eggs, flour, baking soda, chocolate, butter and such and stick a spoon in each one of those ingredients and say "enjoy my cake!" No you show up with a fully baked cake and we enjoy all the flavors and ingredients as we eat the cake. Many people teach based on ingredients, feed them the bread, then break it down for them after they have eaten of it.

Eph 3:
16 That he would grant you, according to the riches of his glory, to be strengthened with might by his Spirit in the inner man; 17 That Christ may dwell in your hearts by faith; that ye, being rooted and grounded in love, 18 May be able to comprehend with all saints what is the breadth, and length, and depth, and height; 19 And to know the love of Christ, which passeth knowledge, that ye might be filled with all the fulness of God.

I want my real me, the inner man to become full. I want to be rooted and grounded as deep as possible in the Love of God. I want to know intimately the Love of Christ and be as full as possible. All of creation is waiting for us to manifest this fullness of the nature and being of God in us.

Eph 5
1 Be ye therefore followers of God, as dear children; 2 And walk in love, as Christ also hath loved us, and hath given himself for us an offering and a sacrifice to God for a sweetsmelling savour.

The Greek word used for followers of God is that word that we mentioned earlier -- mimic. We are to be imitators of God. God is love and that is what we are to be.

Col 3:
14 And above all these things put on charity, which is the bond of perfectness.

The bond of love, I have heard that love is the glue that makes it all stick together. But he uses that word perfectness. We could also say maturity. I want to come into maturity and be all God wants me to be.

2 Tim 1
7 For God hath not given us the spirit of fear; but of power, and of love, and of a sound mind.

We should not fear anything as we have a Spirit of Love. The Spirit of love, the nature and fellowship of the Father. How can we fear anything with Him in us? We are like Job, with a hedge of protection around us. That is if we build that relationship and obey His command to Love. This is not just a name it a claim it thing. You actually have to develop a relationship for any of this to work. You have to get down and personal with God. He wants your heart, all of it, and in return He fills you with His nature and perfection and grace. He surrounds you, soaks you and fills you so fully that nothing about fear has a place in you. People are going to need that in the last days.

1 John 2
15 Love not the world, neither the things that are in the world. If any man love the world, the love of the Father is not in him.

You cannot be sold out to the media and the world way of doing things. The worlds methods have been creeping into the church for several decades, we don't need the world's methods and their traditions. It almost seems as if the world just polished their wares and made them look like gold and the church bought them up. We promote the world's ways in church and yet God has been telling us all along that He does not do things like the World. You cannot straddle the fence. Either be cold and honest about it or be hot. Chose one, we don't need any more lovers of men and the worlds methods in the church.

1John 3
16 Hereby perceive we the love of God, because he laid down his life for us: and we ought to lay down our lives for the brethren. 17 But whoso hath this world's good, and seeth his brother have need, and shutteth up his bowels of compassion from him, how dwelleth the love of God in him?

How do we know we have the love of God in us? Is it just the words we say or is wisdom proved right by her actions? I meet men all the time who want recognition and respect because they have several degrees and such. I tell them the same thing, your testimony is not based on what you say but how you act in the here and now. Today is what matters and today you need to respond to the mercy of God in how you treat others. Once the day ends, start over tomorrow and forget about yesterday. Yesterday can't be changed and tomorrow has any number of possibilities. Today has more than enough to deal with, plenty enough will confront you. The world knows you by your actions, love others and demonstrate your testimony.

1 John 4:7 to 5:3
7 Beloved, let us love one another: for love is of God; and every one that loveth is born of God, and knoweth God. 8 He that loveth not knoweth not God; for God is love. 9 In this was manifested the love of God toward us, because that God sent his only begotten Son into the world, that we might live through him. 10 Herein is love, not that we loved God, but that he loved us, and sent his Son to be the propitiation for our sins. 11 Beloved, if God so loved us, we ought also to love one another.

12 No man hath seen God at any time. If we love one another, God dwelleth in us, and his love is perfected in us. 13 Hereby know we that we dwell in him, and he in us, because he hath given us of his Spirit. 14 And we have seen and do testify that the Father sent the Son to be the Saviour of the world. 15 Whosoever shall confess that Jesus is the Son of God, God dwelleth in him, and he in God. 16 And we have known and believed the love that God hath to us. God is love; and he that dwelleth in love dwelleth in God, and God in him.17 Herein is our love made perfect, that we may have boldness in the day of judgment: because as he is, so are we in this world. 18 There is no fear in love; but perfect love casteth out fear: because fear hath torment. He that feareth is not made perfect in love. 19 We love him, because he first loved us. 20 If a man say, I love God, and hateth his brother, he is a liar: for he that loveth not his brother whom he hath seen, how can he love God whom he hath not seen? 21 And this commandment have we from him, That he who loveth God love his brother also.

Chapter 5
1 Whosoever believeth that Jesus is the Christ is born of God: and every one that loveth him that begat loveth him also that is begotten of him. 2 By this we know that we love the children of God, when we love God, and keep his commandments. 3 For this is the love of God, that we keep his commandments: and his commandments are not grievous.

This section of Scripture is what I like to call the acid test of the believer. Do you say you love God then you have to love others? You must be compassionate and actually care about them. It may not be easy at first but it will grow with in you. Practice the love of God and it gets easier every day. As we love we develop a new nature like His and as we grow it allows us to grow deeper in Him as we develop a new nature. As we grow and the foundation in us grows we can handle more and more. But you have to begin somewhere. You won't be perfect or even good at it in the beginning, but we all have to begin somewhere. You had to crawl before you walked and walk before you ran. Just get started.

2 John 1
5 And now I beseech thee, lady, not as though I wrote a new

commandment unto thee, but that which we had from the beginning, that we love one another. 6 And this is love, that we walk after his commandments. This is the commandment, That, as ye have heard from the beginning, ye should walk in it.

He says, "not as though I wrote you a new command" That is because it has always been. He used the word beginning twice and both are that Greek word Arche, meaning something that was from the beginning. It always was. It always will be. Everlasting to everlasting. Walk in it, walk in love. That is the doctrine of Christ. Love.

You will notice that in almost every scripture reference the writer used Agape as a noun or a pronoun. Agape is the nature of God. 1 John told us that God is love. Now we are speaking about something a little different than the practice and demonstration of Love. Now we are speaking about the nature and the presence of Love. The spirit of God is Love. God is a Spirit. The spirit is Love. You will notice that the Word Agape is so often used in reference to what we become. What we are to be. Not doing but becoming. We are supposed to be reborn and recreated in the image of God, that image is Love. That nature is Love. When God breathed into us He breathed His spirit, His nature in us. That nature was love. Paul told us in Romans 5:5 that the love of God has been shed abroad in our hearts that is the Word agape

Romans 5
5 And hope maketh not ashamed; because the love of God is shed abroad in our hearts by the Holy Ghost which is given unto us.

We could say that this way, the nature and spirit of God was deposited in your heart. We received a portion of Gods nature and Spirit in us when we were born again. What have we done with it? Have we followed after that nature to allow it to become mature and grow? Jesus said even if your faith was like a mustard seed, it could grow to become the biggest of all trees. The nature in you, the seed in you wants to grow and become all it was meant to be. You may want to read "why are the fishermen eating the bait to learn more about trees.

Now let's look at the scriptures specifically that put Agape and Agapao together.

You will notice that when the writer and even Jesus say, love (agapao the practice of and demonstration of love) one another as part of the commandment He then switches to the word Agape, meaning that when we practice the eternal law of love, it produces a nature in us. Paul wrote in Romans, that as we obey the agapao commandment, we become Agape. We step by step and day by day precept by precept, walk in the demonstration of love towards God and others we become transformed into something different. Something we were originally created to be like. Most people have controversy with God because they do not know what the end game is, what is a Christian? What is a person who follows Christ supposed to be like? Love.

As you walk in love (practice and demonstrate on a daily basis towards God and man) you will become what you have practiced. An athlete does not show up on day one of camp and knows the entire game and win. He must practice and try and put forth effort each day to become better and strong and more knowledgeable about the sport he is part of. After time people call him a football player, a baseball player etc.. He became what he practiced. If you do not apply yourself daily you will not become what you were intended to be. You will grow physically older and one day die, but you never become mature in the things of God. Your true nature (the spiritual inner man) never grew up and become what it was created after.

Let's look at some Scripture that show the transformation from a person who is practicing love and then becoming love.

Romans 13:8-10
8 Owe no man any thing, but to love one another: for he that loveth (Agapao) another hath fulfilled the law. 9 For this, Thou shalt not commit adultery, Thou shalt not kill, Thou shalt not steal, Thou shalt not bear false witness, Thou shalt not covet; and if there be any other commandment, it is briefly comprehended in this saying, namely, Thou shalt love(Agapao) thy neighbour as thyself. 10 Love (Agape) worketh no ill to his neighbor: therefore love (Agape) is the fulfilling of the law.

The commandment is verse 8, Agapao and then he switches to the noun Agape in verse 10. Agape becomes the title or the pronoun that the person who follows after love becomes known as.

John 13:34-35

34 A new commandment I give unto you, That ye Agapao one another; as I have Agapao you, that ye also love one another. 35 By this shall all men know that ye are my disciples, if ye have Agape one to another.

The way the world will know you are a disciple or follow of Christ is the Love that will be made manifest in you. Verse 34 is the word agapao and verse 35 is Agape, the nature and development of the presence of God. As Jesus said in John 14 verse 36, He and the Father would manifest or take up residence in us, that residency is the nature and presence of God. The spirit of Love.

2 John 1:

5 And now I beseech thee, lady, not as though I wrote a new commandment unto thee, but that which we had from the beginning, that we Agapao one another. 6 And this is Agape, that we walk after his commandments. This is the commandment, That, as ye have heard from the beginning, ye should walk in it.

He refers to the commandment that was from the beginning Agapeo and then changes to the word Agape, you become what you pursue.

John 14:21-25

21 He that hath my commandments, and keepeth them, he it is that Agapao me: and he that Agapao me shall be Agapao of my Father, and I will love him, and will manifest myself to him. 22 Judas saith unto him, not Iscariot, Lord, how is it that thou wilt manifest thyself unto us, and not unto the world? 23 Jesus answered and said unto him, If a man Agapao me, he will keep my words: and my Father will Aapao him, and we will come unto him, and make our abode with him. 24 He that Agapao me not keepeth not my sayings: and the word which ye hear is not mine, but the Father's which sent me.

Do you love God? Then Obey God. Follow His command. If you do He will move into your life and transformation will begin. Though the word Agape is not in this Scripture the residency of God is! He will abide in you, the temple of the Holy Ghost, the world will know it. You walk in Agapao and He takes up residency in you. You will not only know you are the temple of God but now so will everyone else. You cannot hide God! There will be no faking this! The religious leaders will not appreciate it as it will expose the fake and the dross, but the world is crying out every night for someone to do this. Just obey and walk in love. I know that seems so simple but your sin nature, the fallen nature you have been trained by all your life will fight you step by step. You must renew your nature and fight the good fight. Don't be overly concerned about others and their progress or lack of progress. Your carnal nature will keep you busy enough fighting. Your flesh and your spirit will do battle. The devil will try to keep you overly concerned so as to keep you out of the battle. You can't do what needs to be done straddling the fence, feeding on the world's way and their treats. Focus, discipline your flesh and seek God. The world is looking for those who walk in love, creation is groaning for it. God is glorified when we walk in His love.

John 15
8 Herein is my Father glorified, that ye bear much fruit; so shall ye be my disciples. 9 As the Father hath loved (Agapao) me, so have I loved (Agapao) you: continue ye in my love (Agape). 10 If ye keep my commandments, ye shall abide in my love (Agape) ; even as I have kept my Father's commandments, and abide in his love (Agape) . 11 These things have I spoken unto you, that my joy might remain in you, and that your joy might be full. 12 This is my commandment, That ye love (Agape) one another, as I have loved (Agapao) you. 13 Greater love (Agape) hath no man than this, that a man lay down his life for his friends. 14 Ye are my friends, if ye do whatsoever I command you.

We become His disciples when we walk in love. As we walk in love the nature on the inside of us grows and we become like the Father. Just like Jesus did. We can be full of Joy in walking in love. Jesus is telling us right there how He did it! He obeyed the original law from the beginning and stayed there! He did not get off the narrow path and into the wide easy road, He chose the narrow path and did it! We must do the same.

Gal 5
13 For, brethren, ye have been called unto liberty; only use not

liberty for an occasion to the flesh, but by love (Agape) serve one another. 14 For all the law is fulfilled in one word, even in this; Thou shalt love (Agapao) thy neighbour as thyself.

Use the power, the liberty and the grace of God to pursue God. Not just things you want or need, but things that will edify and uplift others. Use the Spirit of the law of freedom to pursue things to bless others, not just yourself. Now if you just said to yourself, "Well I pay tithes and offerings" Let me tell you the same thing Jesus told the Pharisee's "you've missed the spirit behind the law, you should do those things as well as the latter" This whole Christian experience is a matter of the heart. It is about giving from a heart of love. God so loved He gave.

John 14:19- 22
19 Yet a little while, and the world seeth me no more; but ye see me: because I live, ye shall live also. 20 At that day ye shall know that I am in my Father, and ye in me, and I in you. 21 He that hath my commandments, and keepeth them, he it is that loveth (Agapao) me: and he that loveth (Agapao) me shall be loved (Agapao) of my Father, and I will love (Agapao) him, and will manifest myself to him.22 Judas saith unto him, not Iscariot, Lord, how is it that thou wilt manifest thyself unto us, and not unto the world? 23 Jesus answered and said unto him, If a man love (Demonstrate and practice the act of love towards) me, he will keep my words: and my Father will love (Demonstrate and practice the act of love towards) him, and we will come unto him, and make our abode with him.

This is one of my personal favorites, you obey the command, which is Agapeo, and then God and Jesus will manifest, or take up residency in you. I want that. That is the secret right there. You practice the principle of the eternal law of love and it will cause the Nature of Love to take up residency in you. God is'nt looking for a brick and mortar building to live in, He want to live in us, the temples He made. He wants to reside in us. Wow! People will not cry out against you as they do modern preachers and the 2nd temple, "where is the presence, the glory of God?" If He lives in you and has an address in you, others will know it. It cannot be faked.

I want the presence and nature of God to feel welcome to reside in me. I want Him to do with this temple what He will. I will change the way I walk to become what I was meant to be. It will require all my heart, all my mind soul and emotions and all my physical strength to do it, but He would not have told us to if we could not do it.

Romans 8:19

19 For the earnest expectation of the creature waiteth for the manifestation of the sons of God.

States very clearly that all of creation is waiting for someone to become what they were meant to be. The passage we we walk in love He will manifest Himself in and through us! We become what we were designed to be by practicing and walking in love on a daily basis. We must make it our greatest pursuit and journey in love. Not things, not the getting, not the attention, not the approval of man, but the residency of God in man. Then like Paul says in Ephesians

Eph 3: no longer swayed by the cunning teaching of men but rather becoming mature!

I want to become mature and full with as much of the nature of God as I can. Join me.

BROTHER JOHN

BROTHER JOHN

www.ingramcontent.com/pod-product-compliance
Lightning Source LLC
Chambersburg PA
CBHW071529080526
44588CB00011B/1614